Joint Workshop on NLP&LOD and SWAIE 2013

Semantic Web, Linked Open Data and Information Extraction

Associated with the 9th International Conference on Recent Advances in Natural Language Processing (RANLP 2013)

Hissar, Bulgaria
12 September 2013

ISBN: 978-1-62993-552-2

Printed from e-media with permission by:

Curran Associates, Inc.
57 Morehouse Lane
Red Hook, NY 12571

Some format issues inherent in the e-media version may also appear in this print version.

Printed by Curran Associates, Inc. (2014)

For permission requests, please contact the Association for Computational Linguistics at the address below.

Association for Computational Linguistics
209 N. Eighth Street
Stroudsburg, Pennsylvania 18360

Phone: 1-570-476-8006
Fax: 1-570-476-0860

acl@aclweb.org

Additional copies of this publication are available from:

Curran Associates, Inc.
57 Morehouse Lane
Red Hook, NY 12571 USA
Phone: 845-758-0400
Fax: 845-758-2634
Email: curran@proceedings.com
Web: www.proceedings.com

Introduction

The Linked Open Data (LOD), understood as published structured data, which is interlinked and which builds upon standard Web technologies, such as HTTP and URIs, as well as on RDF-presented world facts datasets in various domains, has become a necessary component within all modern NLP-related tasks and applications since it provides large quantities of useful knowledge about people, facts, organizations, events, etc.

At the same time, the Information Extraction community specialises in mining the nuggets of information from text: such techniques could, however, be enhanced by annotated data or domain-specific resources. The Semantic Web community has already taken great strides in making these resources available through the Linked Open Data cloud, which are now ready for uptake by the Information Extraction community.

The Joint NLP&LOD and SWAIE Workshop presents papers that discuss the above mentioned topics from various perspectives. Enjoy reading them!

The Organizers

Organizers:

NLP&LOD organizers:

Petya Osenova, Sofia University
Kiril Simov, Bulgarian Academy of Sciences
Georgi Georgiev, OntoText Lab
Preslav Nakov, Qatar Computing Research Institute, Qatar Foundation, Qatar

SWAIE organizers:

Diana Maynard, University of Sheffield
Marieke van Erp, VU University Amsterdam
Brian Davis, DERI Galway

Program Committee:

NLP&LOD PC:

Eneko Agirre (University of the Basque Country, Spain)
Isabelle Augenstein (Sheffield University, UK)
Guido Boella (Universitá di Torino, Italy)
Kalina Boncheva (Sheffield University, UK)
António Branco (University of Lisbon, Portugal)
Nicoletta Calzolari (Istituto di Linguistica Computazionale, Italy)
Thierry Declerck (DFKI, Germany)
Georgi Dimitroff (Germany)
Kuzman Ganchev (Google, the USA)
Valia Kordoni (Humboldt University in Berlin, Germany)
Jarred McGinnis (King's College London, UK)
Pavel Mihajlov (Ontotext AD, Bulgaria)
Maciej Piasecki (Wroclaw University of Technology, Poland)
Laura Tolosi (Ontotext AD, Bulgaria)
Gertjan van Noord (University of Groningen, the Netherlands)
Piek Vossen (Vrije Universiteit Amsterdam, the Netherlands)

SWAIE PC:

Eneko Agirre (University of the Basque Country, Spain)
Paul Buitelaar (DERI, Galway, Ireland)
Matje van de Camp (Tilburg University, The Netherlands)
Philipp Cimiano (CITEC University of Bielefeld, Germany)
Hamish Cunningham (University of Sheffield, UK)
Thierry DeClerck (DFKI, Germany)
Antske Fokkens (VU University, the Netherlands)
Dirk Hovy (ISI, USA)
Georgeta Bordea (DERI Galway, Ireland)
Phil Gooch (City University London, UK)

Siegfried Handschuh (DERI, Ireland)
Véronique Malaisé (Elsevier, The Netherlands)
Laurette Pretorius (University of South Africa, South Africa)
German Rigau (University of the Basque Country, Spain)
Marco Rospocher (Fondazione Bruno Kessler, Italy)
Sara Tonelli (Fondazione Bruno Kessler, Italy)
Piek Vossen (VU University, The Netherlands)
René Witte (Concordia University, Montreal, Canada)
Birgit Proell (Johannes Kepler University Linz)
Killian Levacher (KDEG, CNGL)
Chris Welty (IBM, IBM T.J. Watson Research Center in New York)
D.J McCloskey (IBM Watson, IBM Dublin)

Table of Contents

Conference Program

12.09.2013

Session 1: NLP+LOD (Part 1)

(9:15-10:15 (Invited Talk))

Linguistic Linked Open Data (LLOD) – Building the cloud
Christian Chiarcos

(10:15-10:45)

Evaluation of SPARQL query generation from natural language questions
K. Bretonnel Cohen and Jin-Dong Kim

Session 2: NLP+LOD (Part 2)

(11:15-11:45)

Mining translations from the web of open linked data
John Philip McCrae and Philipp Cimiano

(11:45-12:15)

Porting Elements of the Austrian Baroque Corpus onto the Linguistic Linked Open Data Format
Ulrike Czeitschner, Thierry Declerck and Claudia Resch

(12:15-12:45)

Towards a System for Dynamic Language Resources in LOD
Kiril Simov

12.09.2013 (continued)

Session 3: SWAIE (Part 1)

(14:00-15:00 (Invited Talk))

Applications of Semantic Publishing
Borislav Popov

(15:00-15:30)

Literature-driven Curation for Taxonomic Name Databases
Hui Yang, Alistair Willis, David Morse and Anne De Roeck

(15:30-16:00)

Exploring the inference role in automatic information extraction from texts
Denis de Araujo, Sandro Rigo, Carolina Muller and Rove Chishman

Session 4: SWAIE (Part 2)

(16:30-17:00)

Combined analysis of news and Twitter messages
Mian Du, Jussi Kangasharju, Ossi Karkulahti, Lidia Pivovarova and Roman Yangarber

(17:00-18:00 (Invited Talk))

Linguistically analyzed labels of knowledge objects: How can they support OBIE? Lessons learned from the Monnet and TrendMiner projects
Thierry Declerck

Linguistic Linked Open Data (LLOD) – Building the cloud

Christian Chiarcos
Goethe-University Frankfurt am Main, Germany
chiarcos@informatik.uni-frankfurt.de

The last decades have seen an immense maturation of Natural Language Processing (NLP) and an increased interest to apply NLP techniques and resources to real-world applications in business and academia. This process has certainly been facilitated by the increased availability of language data in the internet age, and the subsequent paradigm shift to statistical approaches, but also it coincided with an increasing acceptance of empirical approaches in linguistics and related academic fields, including empirical approaches to typology (Greenberg, 1963), corpus linguistics (Francis and Kucera, 1979, Brown Corpus), and (computational) lexicography (Kucera, 1969), as well as the dawn of Digital Humanities (Busa, 1974).

Given the complexity of language and the analysis of linguistic data on different levels, its investigation involves a broad band-width of formalisms and resources used to analyze, process and generate natural language. With the transition to empirical, data-driven research, the primary challenge in the field is thus to store, connect and exploit the wealth of language data available in all its heterogeneity. **Interoperability** of language resources has hence been an important issue addressed by the community since the late 1980s (Text Encoding Initiative, 1990), but still remains a problem that is solved only partially, i.e., on the level of specific sub-types of linguistic resources, such as lexical resources (Francopoulo et al., 2006) or annotated corpora (Ide and Suderman, 2007), respectively. A closely related challenge is **information integration**, i.e., how information from different sources can be retrieved and combined in an efficient way.

Recently, both challenges have been addressed by means of Linked Data principles (Chiarcos et al., 2013a,b), eventually leading to the formation of a **Linguistic Linked Open Data (LLOD) cloud** (Chiarcos et al., 2012b). The talk describes its current state of development, it presents selected examples for main types of linguistic resources in the LLOD cloud, and objectives leading to the adaptation of Linked Data principles for any of these.

Further, the talk elaborates on history and goals behind this effort, its relation to established standardization initiatives in the field, and on-going community activities conducted under the umbrella of the **Open Linguistics Working Group (OWLG)** of the Open Knowledge Foundation (Chiarcos et al., 2012a), an initiative of experts from various fields concerned with linguistic data, which works towards

1. promoting the idea of open linguistic resources,
2. developing means for their representation, and
3. encouraging the exchange of ideas and resources across different disciplines.

As the Linked Data paradigm can be used to facilitate any of these aspects, the OWLG identified potential application scenarios for linked and/or open resources in linguistics since its formation in 2010. The Working Group also has intensified its **community-building efforts** by means of a series of workshops, accompanying publications and data set releases. As a result of this process, numerous resources have been provided in a Linked-Data-compliant way, and linked with each other, as sketched here for selected examples.

References

Roberto Busa. *Index Thomisticus*. Frommann-Holzboog, Stuttgart, 1974.

Christian Chiarcos, Sebastian Hellmann, Sebastian Nordhoff, Steven Moran, Richard Littauer, Judith Eckle-Kohler, Iryna Gurevych, Silvana Hartmann, Michael Matuschek, and Christian

M. Meyer. The Open Linguistics Working Group. In *Proc. 8th International Conference on Language Resources and Evaluation (LREC-2012)*, pages 3603–3610, Istanbul, Turkey, May 2012a.

Christian Chiarcos, Sebastian Nordhoff, and Sebastian Hellmann. *Linked Data in Linguistics. Representing and Connecting Language Data and Language Metadata*. Springer, Heidelberg, 2012b.

Christian Chiarcos, John McCrae, Philipp Cimiano, and Christiane Fellbaum. Towards open data for linguistics: Lexical Linked Data. In Alessandro Oltramari, Piek Vossen, Lu Qin, and Eduard Hovy, editors, *New Trends of Research in Ontologies and Lexical Resources*. Springer, Heidelberg, 2013a.

Christian Chiarcos, Steven Moran, Pablo N. Mendes, Sebastian Nordhoff, and Richard Littauer. Building a Linked Open Data cloud of linguistic resources: Motivations and developments. In Iryna Gurevych and Jungi Kim, editors, *The People's Web Meets NLP. Collaboratively Constructed Language Resources*. Springer, Heidelberg, 2013b.

W. Nelson Francis and Henry Kucera. *Brown Corpus Manual. Manual of Information to accompany A Standard Corpus of Present-Day Edited American English, for use with Digital Computers*. Providence, Rhode Island, 1979. URL `\url{http://icame.uib.no/brown/bcm.html}`. original edition 1964.

Gil Francopoulo, Monte George, Nicoletta Calzolari, Monica Monachini, Nuria Bel, Mandy Pet, and Claudia Soria. Lexical Markup Framework (LMF). In *Proc. 5th International Conference on Language Resources and Evaluation (LREC-2006)*, Genoa, May 2006.

Joseph Greenberg. Some universals of grammar with particular reference to the order of meaningful elements. In Joseph Greenberg, editor, *Universals of Language*, pages 58–90. MIT Press, Cambridge, 1963.

Nancy Ide and Keith Suderman. GrAF: A graph-based format for linguistic annotations. In *Proc. 1st Linguistic Annotation Workshop (LAW 2007)*, pages 1–8, Prague, Czech Republic, Jun 2007.

Henry Kucera. Computers in language analysis and lexicography. In *American Heritage Dictionary of the English Language*, pages XXXVII–XL. Houghton Mifflin, New York, 1969.

Text Encoding Initiative. TEI P1 guidelines for the encoding and interchange of machine readable texts. `http://www.tei-c.org/Vault/Vault-GL.html`, Nov 1990. draft version 1.1 1.

Evaluation of SPARQL query generation from natural language questions

K. Bretonnel Cohen
Computational Bioscience Program
U. Colorado School of Medicine

Jin-Dong Kim
Database Center for Life Science

Abstract

SPARQL queries have become the standard for querying linked open data knowledge bases, but SPARQL query construction can be challenging and time-consuming even for experts. SPARQL query generation from natural language questions is an attractive modality for interfacing with LOD. However, how to evaluate SPARQL query generation from natural language questions is a mostly open research question. This paper presents some issues that arise in SPARQL query generation from natural language, a test suite for evaluating performance with respect to these issues, and a case study in evaluating a system for SPARQL query generation from natural language questions.

1 Introduction

The SPARQL query language is the standard for retrieving linked open data from triple stores. SPARQL is powerful, flexible, and allows the use of RDF, with all of its advantages over traditional databases. However, SPARQL query construction has been described as "absurdly difficult" (McCarthy et al., 2012), and even experienced users may struggle with it. For this reason, various methods have been suggested for aiding in SPARQL query generation, including assisted query construction (McCarthy et al., 2012) and, most germaine to this work, converting natural language questions into SPARQL queries.

Although a body of work on SPARQL query generation from natural language questions has been growing, no consensus has yet developed about how to evaluate such systems. (Abacha and Zweigenbaum, 2012) evaluated their system by manual inspection of the SPARQL queries that they generated. No gold standard was prepared—the authors examined each query and determined whether or not it accurately represented the original natural language question. (Yahya et al., 2012) used two human judges to manually examine the output of their system at three points—disambiguation, SPARQL query construction, and the answers returned. If the judges disagreed, a third judge examined the output. (McCarthy et al., 2012) does not have a formal evaluation, but rather gives two examples of the output of the SPARQL Assist system. (This is not a system for query generation from natural language questions per se, but rather an application for assisting in query constructions through methods like auto-completion suggestions.) (Unger et al., 2012) is evaluated on the basis of a gold standard of answers from a static data set. It is not clear how (Lopez et al., 2007) is evaluated, although they give a nice classification of error types. Reviewing this body of work, the trends that have characterized most past work are that either systems are not formally evaluated, or they are evaluated in a functional, black-box fashion, examining the mapping between inputs and one of two types of outputs—either the SPARQL queries themselves, or the answers returned by the SPARQL queries. The significance of the work reported here is that it attempts to develop a unified methodology for evaluating systems for SPARQL query generation from natural language questions that meets a variety of desiderata for such a methodology and that is generalizable to other systems besides our own.

In the development of our system for SPARQL query generation from natural language questions, it became clear that we needed a robust approach to system evaluation. The approach needed to meet a number of desiderata:

- Automatability: It should be possible to automate tests so that they can be run automatically many times during the day and so that there is no opportunity for humans to miss errors when doing manual examination.

- Granularity: The approach should allow for granular evaluation of behavior—that is, rather than (or in addition to) just returning a single metric that characterizes performance over an entire data set, such as accuracy, it should allow for evaluation of functionality over specific types of inputs.
- Modularity: The approach should allow for evaluating individual modules of the system independently.
- Functionality: The approach should allow functional, black-box evaluation of the end-to-end performance of the system as a whole.

The hypothesis being explored in the work reported here is that it is possible to conduct a principled fine-grained evaluation of software for SPARQL query generation from natural language questions that is effective in uncovering weaknesses in the software.

As in any software testing situation, various methods of evaluating the software exist. A typical black-box approach would be to establish a gold standard of the SPARQL queries themselves, and/or of the answers that should be returned in response to a natural language question.. However, we ruled out applying the black-box approach to the SPARQL queries themselves because there are multiple correct SPARQL queries that are equivalent in terms of the triples that they will return from a linked open data source. We ruled out a black-box approach based entirely on examining the triples returned from the query when the SPARQL query was executed against the triple store because the specific list of triples is subject to change unpredictably as the contents of the triple store are updated by the data maintainers.

We opted for a gray-box approach, in which we examine the output at multiple stages of processing. The first was at the point of mapping to TUIs. The Unified Medical Language System's Semantic Network contains a hierarchically grouped set of 133 semantic types, each with a Type Unique Identifier (TUI). That is, for any given natural language question that should cause a mapping to a TUI, we examined if a TUI was generated by the system and, if so, if it was the correct TUI. The second was the point of SPARQL query generation, where we focused on syntactic validity, rather than the entire SPARQL query (for the reason given above). We also examined the output of the SPARQL query, but not in terms of exact match to a gold standard. In practice, the queries would typically return a long list of triples, and the specific list of triples is subject to change unpredictably as the contents of the triple store are updated by the OMIM maintainers. For that reason, we have focused on ensuring that we know one correct triple which should occur in the output, and validating the presence of that triple in the output. We have also inspected the output for triples that we knew from domain expertise should not be returned, although we have done that manually so far and have not formalized it in the test suite.

In this paper, we focus on one specific aspect of the gray-box evaluation: the mapping to TUIs. As will be seen, mapping to TUIs when appropriate, and of course to the correct TUI, is an important feature of answering domain-specific questions. As we developed our system beyond the initial prototype, it quickly became apparent that there was a necessity to differentiate between elements of the question that referred to specific entities in the triple store, and elements of the question that referred to general semantic categories. For example, for queries like *What genes are related to heart disease?*, we noticed that *heart disease* was being mapped to the correct entity in the triple store, but *genes*, rather than being treated as a general category, was also being mapped (erroneously) to a particular instance in the triple store. Given the predicates in the triple store, the best solution was to recognize general categories in questions and map them to TUIs. Therefore, we developed a method to recognize general categories in questions and map them to TUIs. Testing this functionality is the main topic of this paper.

2 Materials and methods

2.1 Online Mendelian Inheritance In Man

In this work we focused on a single linked open data source, known as Online Mendelian Inheritance in Man (OMIM) (Amberger et al., 2011).

The most obvious application of OMIM, and the one that biomedical researchers are most accustomed to using it for, is queries about genes and diseases, but this is a **much** richer resource that is probably not often exploited to the full extent that it could be; in fact, the web-based interface offers no options at all for exploiting it beyond querying for genes and diseases.

The knowledge model goes far beyond this. It includes linkages between at least 12 semantic types, listed below in the Results section. OMIM makes use of TUIs in typing the participants in many of the triples that it encodes. In particular, each of the linkages described above is actually a pair of TUIs.

2.2 LODQA

To understand the evaluation methodology that we developed, it is helpful to understand the system under test. A prototype version of the system that differed from the current system primarily in terms of not performing TUI identification and of using a default relation for all predicates is described in some detail in (Kim and Cohen, 2013). We briefly describe the current version of the system here.

2.2.1 Architecture

In order both to understand what features of our system need to be tested and to understand how well the testing approach will generalize to evaluating other systems for SPARQL query generation from natural language questions, it is helpful to understand, in general terms, the architecture of the system that we are testing. The primary modules of the system are as follows:

- A dependency parser for determining semantic relations in the question.
- A base noun chunker for finding terms that need to be mapped to entities or TUIs in the linked open data set.
- A system for matching base noun chunks to entities or TUIs in the linked open data set.
- A module for presudo-SPARQL generation.
- A module for generating the final SPARQL query.

The user enters a question in natural language and selects a linked open data source to be queried. The first step is production of a dependency parse, using a version of the Enju parser that was trained on a corpus of English-language questions. This parse is used to identify the "target" of the question, e.g. the *wh*-NP *genes* in *What genes are associated with heart failure?* Base noun chunks are then extracted using a pattern-based approach. A pseudo-SPARQL query is generated, using the base noun chunks. TUIs are identified. The REST API of the OntoFinder system is then used to identify entities from the relevant linked open data source. For example, with OMIM selected as the linked open data source, in the query *What genes are associated with congestive heart failure?*, the base noun chunk *genes* is mapped to the TUI *T028* and the base noun chunk *congestive heart failure* is mapped to the OMIM entity *MTHU005753*. Finally, the full SPARQL query is generated, including the appropriate relation type.

2.3 A test suite for LODQA and OMIM

To build the test suite, we used three strategies: exploring a single disease in depth, sampling a variety of topics from a broad domain, and exploring linguistic variability. We began by selecting a disease represented in OMIM that had links to a wide variety of semantic types—Kearns-Sayre syndrome, a syndrome associated with ophthalmoplegia, pigmentary degeneration of the retina, and cardiomyopathy, caused by mitochondrial deletions (Kearns, 1965). For a broad domain, we chose cardiology, since one of the authors has extensive experience in that clinical area.

We accessed the entry for Kearns-Sayre syndrome through the National Center for Biomedical Ontology BioPortal. To obtain a representative sample of TUIs, we exhaustively followed all links in the RO field. We then constructed at least one pair of questions for each pair of semantic types—one that required recognizing the *type* of the TUI, and one that required recognizing an *instance* of an entity with that TUI. For example, for the TUI *Congenital Abnormality*, we constructed the questions *What congenital abnormalities are associated with Kearns-Sayre syndrome?* (type) and *What diseases is microcephaly associated with?* (where *microcephaly* is an entity of type *Congenital Abnormality*). We then explored the CHD field, yielding two additional TUIs. 10 of the TUIs could reasonably be expected to occur in natural questions (details below), and we built questions for all of these.

3 Results

The strategy described above resulted in a set of 38 natural language questions. Since the point of a test suite is to uncover problems, we focus here on the ability of the test suite to find problems, rather than focusing on how many tests we passed.

Within the set of triples for Kearns-Sayre syndrome, we found the following types of relations:

- Disease or Syndrome → Anatomical Abnormality
- Disease or Syndrome → Finding
- Disease or Syndrome → Functional Concept
- Disease or Syndrome → Disease or Syndrome
- Disease or Syndrome → Sign or Symptom
- Disease or Syndrome → Congenital Abnormality
- Disease or Syndrome → Mental or Behavioral Dysfunction
- Disease or Syndrome → Cell or Molecular Dysfunction
- Disease or Syndrome → Body Part, Organ, or Organ Component
- Disease or Syndrome → Clinical Attribute
- Disease or Syndrome → Qualitative Concept
- Disease or Syndrome → Pathologic Function

Of these twelve TUIs, 10 had forms from which one could produce a natural-sounding natural language question, the exceptions being *Functional Concept* and *Qualitative Concept*. Out of 10 TUIs that we tested, we were able to find problems with 3 of them. The problems ranged from failures to recognize TUIs to crashing the system.

Although there is as yet no non-application-specific taxonomy of error types in the task of SPARQL query generation from natural language questions (although see (Lopez et al., 2007) for an application-specific one), a number of categories that should appear in such a taxonomy presented themselves in the results of our tests:

- Number disagreements between the canonical form in the triple store and the most natural form in natural language. For example, concepts most commonly occur in the names of TUIs in singular form, e.g. *Gene or Genome*, but are more likely to occur in natural language questions in the plural, e.g. *What genes are associated with cystic fibrosis?*
- Various forms of conjunctive and disjunctive coordination, often with the potential for scope ambiguity. The most natural form of the TUI *Sign or Symptom* in a natural language question is *What signs* ***and*** *symptoms*, and this form caused the application to crash.
- Discrepancies between part of speech in the canonical form in the triple store and the most natural form in natural language. For example, the TUI *Cell or molecular dysfunction* is more likely to appear in natural language as *cellular dysfunction* than as *cell dysfunction*; these more natural forms were not recognized.

4 Discussion and conclusions

Initial exploration of a linked open data source is likely to reveal issues that must be resolved in order for natural language processing techniques to succeed. In our case, an immediate challenge that presented itself was recognizing when noun phrases should be mapped to TUIs, rather than being mapped to entities in the knowledge base.

Having recognized an issue to be resolved, test suites can be constructed to evaluate how well the issue is handled. In our case, this meant determining the full range of interacting TUIs in the knowledge base through manual exploration of the data, and then constructing a test suite that contained strings that should map to these TUIs, with the full range of linguistic variation that they can manifest.

A reasonable question to ask is whether this methodology is generalizable. Although it remains to be demonstrated, we suspect that it is, in two directions. The first is generalization to other linked open data sources. It seems likely that the methodology will generalize to the many biomedical linked open data sources in the National Center for Biomedical Ontology BioPortal. The second is generalization to other systems for SPARQL query generation from natural language questions. Based on a review of related work, we suspect that the methodology could be applied with very little adaptation to the systems described in (Lopez et al., 2007), (Abacha and Zweigenbaum, 2012), and (Yahya et al., 2012), which all have architectures that lend themselves to the type of gray-box evaluation that we have done here.

Future work will extend in a variety of directions. Following the test-driven development paradigm, further construction of the test suite will proceed ahead of the development of the LODQA application. Pressing issues for future development as we evolve further in the continuum from prototype proof-of-concept to fully-functioning application are automatic determination of the relation between the subject and object; handling negation; and handling questions that require querying multiple triple stores.

References

Asma Ben Abacha and Pierre Zweigenbaum. 2012. Medical question answering: translating medical questions into SPARQL queries. In *Proceedings of the 2nd ACM SIGHIT International Health Informatics Symposium*, pages 41–50.

Joanna Amberger, Carol Bocchini, and Ada Hamosh. 2011. A new face and new challenges for Online Mendelian Inheritance in Man (OMIM®). *Human Mutation*, 32(5):564–567.

T.P. Kearns. 1965. External ophthalmoplegia, pigmentary degeneration of the retina, and cardiomyopathy: a newly recognized syndrome. *Transactions of the Ophthalmological Society of the United Kingdom*, 63:559–625.

Jin-Dong Kim and K.B̃retonnel Cohen. 2013. Natural language query processing for SPARQL generation: A prototype system for SNOMED CT. In *Proceedings of BioLINK 2013: Roles for text mining in biomedical knowledge discovery and translational medicine*, pages 32–38.

Vanessa Lopez, Victoria Uren, Enrico Motta, and Michele Pasin. 2007. AquaLog: An ontology-driven question answering system for organizational semantic intranets. *Journal of Web Semantics*.

Luke McCarthy, Ben Vandervalk, and Mark Wilkinson. 2012. SPARQL Assist language-neutral query composer. *BMC Bioinformatics*, 13.

Christina Unger, Lorenz Bühmann, Jens Lehmann, Axel-Cyrille Ngonga Ngomo, Daniel Gerber, and Philipp Cimiano. 2012. Template-based question answering over RDF data. In *Proceedings of the 21st international conference on World Wide Web*, pages 639–648.

Mohamed Yahya, Klaus Berberich, Shady Elbassuoni, Maya Ramanath, Volker Tresp, and Gerhard Weikum. 2012. Natural language questions for the web of data. In *Proceedings of the 2012 Joint Conference on Empirical Methods in Natural Language Processing and Computational Natural Language Learning*, pages 379–390.

Mining translations from the web of open linked data

John Philip McCrae
University of Bielefeld
jmccrae@cit-ec.uni-bielefeld.de

Philipp Cimiano
University of Bielefeld
cimiano@cit-ec.uni-bielefeld.de

Abstract

In this paper we consider the prospect of extracting translations for words from the web of linked data. By searching for entities that have labels in both English and German we extract 665,000 translations. We then also consider a linguistic linked data resource, lemonUby, from which we extract a further 115,000 translations. We combine these translations with the Moses statistical machine translation, and we show that the translations extracted from the linked data can be used to improve the translation of unknown words.

1 Introduction

In recent years there has been a massive explosion in the amount and quality of data available as linked data on the web. This data frequently describes entities in multiple languages and as such can be used as a source of translations. In particular, the web contains much data about named entities, such as locations, films, people and so forth, and often these named entities have translations in many languages. In this paper, we address the question of what can be achieved by using the large amounts of data available as multilingual Linked Open Data (LOD). As state-of-the-art statistical machine translation systems (Koehn, 2010) are typically trained on outdated or out-of-domain parallel corpora such as on the transcripts of the European Parliament (Koehn, 2005), we expect to increase the coverage of domain-specific terminology.

In addition, there has recently been a move towards the publication of of language resources using linked data principles (Chiarcos et al., 2011), which can be expected to lead to a significant increase the availability of information relevant to NLP on the Web. In particular, the representation of legacy resources such as Wiktionary and OmegaWiki on the web of data should ameliorate the process of harvesting translations from these resources.

We consider two sources for translations from linked data: firstly, we consider mining labels for concepts from the data contained in the 2010 Billion Triple Challenge (BTC) data set, as well as DBpedia (Auer et al., 2007) and FreeBase (Bollacker et al., 2008). Secondly, we mine translations from lemonUby (Eckle-Kohler et al., 2013), a resource that integrates a number of distinct dictionary language resources in the *lemon* (Lexicon Model for Ontologies) format (McCrae et al., 2012), which is a model for representing rich lexical information including forms, sense, morphology and syntax of ontology labels. We then consider the process of including these extra translations into an existing translation system, namely Moses (Koehn et al., 2007). We show that we can extract many translations which are complementary to those found by the statistical machine translation system and that these translations improve the translation performance of the system.

2 Mining translations from the linked open data cloud

Obtaining translations from the Linked Open Data (LOD) cloud is a non-trivial task as there are many different properties used to specify the label or name of resources on the LOD. The standard method of identifying the language of a label is by means of the `xml:lang` annotation, which should be an ISO-639 code, such as "en" or "eng" for English. As noted by Ell et al. (2011), very little of the data found on the web actually has such a language tag. Further, as the labels are typically short it is very difficult to infer the language reliably based on its surface form. As such we are compelled to rely on the language tags, and this means that from the data we can only recover a small amount of what may be available. In particular, out of the Billion Triple Challenge data we recover approximately 398 million labels in English but only 144,000 labels in German. Unsurprisingly, given the dominance of English on the web of data (Gracia et al., 2012), we find that there are many more labels in English. We then filter these two sets so that we keep only URIs for which there is both an English and a German label. Among this data is a significant number of long textual descriptions, which are very unlikely to be useful for translation, such that we also filter out all labels whose length is more than 10 characters. This filter was necessary to reduce the amount of noisy "translations". We do not filter according to any particular property, e.g., we do not limit ourselves to the RDFS label property, but in the case where we have multiple labels on the same entity we select the RDFS label property as a preference.

In addition to the BTC data, we also include two large resources for which there are multilingual labels in their entirety. These resources are DBpedia[1] and FreeBase[2] as these resources contain many labels in many languages. As the resources are consistent in the use of the rdfs:label property, we extract translations by looking at the rdfs:label property and the language tag. In Table 1 we see the number of translations that we extract from the three resources. We see that we extract fewer resources from the BTC data but a large and reasonable number of translations from the other two resources

3 Translations mined from linguistic linked data

For finding translations from linguistic linked data, we focus on the lemonUby (Eckle-Kohler et al., 2013) resource, which is a linked data version of the UBY resource (Gurevych et al., 2012). This resource contains *lemon* versions of a number of resources in particular:

- FrameNet (Baker et al., 1998)
- OmegaWiki [3]
- VerbNet (Schuler, 2005)
- Wiktionary [4]
- WordNet (Fellbaum, 2010)

[1]We use the dump of the 3.5 version

[2]The dump was downloaded on June 21st 2013

[3]http://omegawiki.org

[4]http://www.wiktionary.org

Resource	Translations
OmegaWiki (English)	56,077
OmegaWiki (German)	55,990
Wiktionary (English)	34,421
Wiktionary (German)	43,212
All	114,644
lemonUby and cloud	777,173

Table 2: Number of translations extracted for linguistic linked data resource lemonUby

Out of these resources, FrameNet, VerbNet and WordNet are monolingual English resources, so we focus on the OmegaWiki and Wiktionary part of the resources. LemonUby contains direct translations on the lexical senses of many of the resources (see Figure 1 for an example). The total number of translations extracted for each subresource is given in Table 2 as well as the results in combination with the number of translation extracted from labels in the previous section.

4 Exploiting mined translations mined from linked data

In order evaluate the utility of the translations extracted from the linked data cloud, we integrate them into the phrase table of the Moses system (Koehn et al., 2007) trained on Europarl data (Koehn, 2005). We used the system primarily in an 'off-the-shelf' manner in order to focus on the effect of adding the linked data translations.

Moses uses a log-linear model as the baseline for its translations, where translations are generated by a decoder and evaluated according to the following model:

$$p(\mathbf{t}|\mathbf{f}) = \exp(\sum_i \phi_i(\mathbf{t}, \mathbf{f}))$$

Where $\mathbf{t}$ is the candidate translation sentence, $\mathbf{f}$ is the input foreign text and ϕ_i are scoring functions. In the phrase-based model the translation is derived compositionally by considering phrases and their translations stored in the so called *phrase table* of the Moses system.

The main challenge in integrating these translations derived from linked data lies in the fact that they lack a probability score. For each translation pair (a, b) derived from the linked data, we distinguish two cases: If the translation is already in the phrase table, we add a new feature that is set to 1.0 to indicate that the translation was found

Resource	English Labels	German Labels	Translations
BTC	398,902,866	144,226	51,756
DBpedia	7,332,616	590,381	540,134
FreeBase	41,261,806	1,654,254	259,923
All	447,497,288	2,338,861	665,910

Table 1: The number of labels and translations found in the linked data cloud by resource

```
<OW_eng_LexicalEntry_0#CanonicalForm> lemon:writtenRep "rain"@eng.
<OW_eng_LexicalEntry_0> lemon:canonicalForm <OW_eng_LexicalEntry_0#CanonicalForm> ;
  lemon:sense <OW_eng_Sense_0> .
<OW_eng_Sense_0> uby:equivalent "schiffen"@deu ,
  "regnen"@deu .
```

Figure 1: An example of the relevant data for a *lemon* lexical entry from the OmegaWiki English section of lemonUby

	BLEU	Evaluator 1	Evaluator 2
Baseline	11.80	36%	34%
+LD	11.78	64%	64%

Table 3: The comparative evaluation of the translations with and without linked data

from the Linked Data Cloud. If the translation was not in the phrase table, we add a new entry with probability 1.0 for all scores and the feature for linked data set to 1.0. For all other translations, the feature indicating provenance from the Linked Data Cloud is set to 0.0. The weights for the log-linear model are learned using the MERT system (Och, 2003). As such we do not use the linked data itself to choose between different translation candidates but rely on the methods built into the machine translations system, in particular the language model.

5 Results

We extracted the baseline phrase table, reordering and language model from version 7 of the EuroParl corpus translating from English to German. In order to evaluate the impact of Linked Data translations on translation quality, we rely on the News Commentary 2011 corpus provided as part of the WMT-12 translation task (Callison-Burch et al., 2012). We found that 25,688 translations from the linked data were relevant to this corpus of which 22,291 (87%) were out of the vocabulary of EuroParl. We used MERT to learn the parameters of the model and observed that the weighting for the linked data feature was negative, indicating that the translations from the linked data improved the translation quality almost exclusively in the case that the machine translation system did not have an existing candidate. We then generated all translations for the baseline system without any linked data translations and for the system augmented with all the linked data translations. Out of 3,003 translations in the test set, we found 346 translations which were changed by the introduction of linked data translation. For each translation, we performed a manual evaluation with two evaluators. They were both presented with 50 translations, one with linked data and one without linked data and asked to choose the best one ("no opinion" was also allowed). The translations were presented in a random order and there was no indication which system they came from so this experiment was performed blind. The evaluators were a native English speaker, who is fluent in German, and a native German speaker, who is fluent in English, and had a Cohen's Kappa Agreement of 0.56. In addition, we calculated BLEU (Papineni et al., 2002) scores. The results are presented in Table 3.

The results show that there is very little change in BLEU scores but the manual evaluation reveals that there was an improvement in quality of the translations. We believe the BLEU scores did not correlate with the manual evaluation due to the fact that many of the translations harvested from the linked data cloud were longer on the German side than the English side, for example the English "RPG" was translated as "Papier-und-Bleistift Rollenspiele", which was not in the reference translation.

6 Conclusion

In this paper we investigated the impact of integrating translations harvested from the Linked Open Data cloud into a state-of-the-art statistical machine translation system. We have shown that it is possible to harvest a large number of translations from the LOD. Furthermore, we found that the task was further enabled by the current growth in linguistic linked data represented in models such as *lemon*. We then integrated these extracted translations into the phrase table of a statistical machine translation system and found that the usage of linked data was most appropriate for terms that were out of the vocabulary of the machine translation system. One of the key challenges in extracting and exploiting such translations is to appropriately capture the context of these translations allow for selecting what kind of linked data may be effective for a given translation task. This will be addressed in future work.

Acknowledgments

This work was funded by the PortDial project under the EU Seventh Framework Programme (FP7), grant number 296170. We would like to thank Sebastian Walter for his help in the experiments.

References

Sören Auer, Christian Bizer, Georgi Kobilarov, Jens Lehmann, Richard Cyganiak, and Zachary Ives. 2007. Dbpedia: A nucleus for a web of open data. In *The Semantic Web, 6th International Semantic Web Conference, 2nd Asian Semantic Web Conference*, pages 722–735. Springer.

Collin F Baker, Charles J Fillmore, and John B Lowe. 1998. The Berkeley FrameNet project. In *Proceedings of the 17th International Conference on Computational Linguistics*, pages 86–90.

Kurt Bollacker, Colin Evans, Praveen Paritosh, Tim Sturge, and Jamie Taylor. 2008. Freebase: a collaboratively created graph database for structuring human knowledge. In *Proceedings of the 2008 ACM SIGMOD international conference on Management of data*, pages 1247–1250.

Chris Callison-Burch, Philipp Koehn, Christof Monz, Matt Post, Radu Soricut, and Lucia Specia. 2012. Findings of the 2012 workshop on statistical machine translation. In *Proceedings of the Seventh Workshop on Statistical Machine Translation*, pages 10–51.

Christian Chiarcos, Sebastian Hellmann, and Sebastian Nordhoff. 2011. Towards a linguistic linked open data cloud: The open linguistics working group. *TAL*, 52(3):245–275.

Judith Eckle-Kohler, John McCrae, and Christian Chiarcos. 2013. lemonUby-a large, interlinked, syntactically-rich resource for ontologies. *Semantic Web Journal, submitted. special issue on Multilingual Linked Open Data.*

Basil Ell, Denny Vrandečić, and Elena Simperl. 2011. Labels in the web of data. In *The Semantic Web, 10th International Semantic Web Conference*, pages 162–176.

Christiane Fellbaum. 2010. *WordNet*. Springer.

Jorge Gracia, Elena Montiel-Ponsoda, Philipp Cimiano, Asunción Gómez-Pérez, Paul Buitelaar, and John McCrae. 2012. Challenges for the multilingual web of data. *Web Semantics: Science, Services and Agents on the World Wide Web*, 11:63–71.

Iryna Gurevych, Judith Eckle-Kohler, Silvana Hartmann, Michael Matuschek, Christian M Meyer, and Christian Wirth. 2012. Uby: A large-scale unified lexical-semantic resource based on LMF. In *Proceedings of the 13th Conference of the European Chapter of the Association for Computational Linguistics*, pages 580–590.

Philipp Koehn, Hieu Hoang, Alexandra Birch, Chris Callison-Burch, Marcello Federico, Nicola Bertoldi, Brooke Cowan, Wade Shen, Christine Moran, Richard Zens, et al. 2007. Moses: Open source toolkit for statistical machine translation. In *Proceedings of the 45th Annual Meeting of the ACL*, pages 177–180.

Philipp Koehn. 2005. Europarl: A parallel corpus for statistical machine translation. In *MT summit*, volume 5.

Philipp Koehn. 2010. *Statistical Machine Translation*. Cambridge University Press.

John McCrae, Guadalupe Aguado-de Cea, Paul Buitelaar, Philipp Cimiano, Thierry Declerck, Asunción Gómez-Pérez, Jorge Gracia, Laura Hollink, Elena Montiel-Ponsoda, Dennis Spohr, et al. 2012. Interchanging lexical resources on the semantic web. *Language Resources and Evaluation*, 46(4):701–719.

Franz Josef Och. 2003. Minimum error rate training in statistical machine translation. In *Proceedings of the 41st Annual Meeting on Association for Computational Linguistics-Volume 1*, pages 160–167.

Kishore Papineni, Salim Roukos, Todd Ward, and Wei-Jing Zhu. 2002. Bleu: a method for automatic evaluation of machine translation. In *Proceedings of the 40th annual meeting on association for computational linguistics*, pages 311–318.

Karin Kipper Schuler. 2005. *VerbNet: A broad-coverage, comprehensive verb lexicon*. Ph.D. thesis, University of Colorado Boulder.

Porting Elements of the Austrian Baroque Corpus onto the Linguistic Linked Open Data Format

Ulrike Czeitschner
Institute for Corpus Linguistics and Text Technology
Austrian Academy of Sciences
Ulrike.Czeitschner@oeaw.ac.at

Thierry Declerck
German Research Center for Artificial Intelligence, GmbH
thierry.declerck@dfki.de

Claudia Resch
Institute for Corpus Linguistics and Text Technology
Austrian Academy of Sciences
Claudia.Resch@oeaw.ac.at

Abstract

We describe work on porting linguistic and semantic annotation applied to the Austrian Baroque Corpus (ABaC:us) to a format supporting its publication in the Linked Open Data Framework. This work includes several aspects, like a derived lexicon of old forms used in the texts and their mapping to modern German lemmas, the description of morpho-syntactic features and the building of domain-specific controlled vocabularies for covering the semantic aspects of this historical corpus. As a central and recurrent topic in the texts is death and dying, a first step in our work was geared towards the establishment of a death-related taxonomy. In order to provide for linguistic information to their textual content, labels of the taxonomy are pointing to linked data in the field of language resources.

1 Introduction

ABaC:us[1] is a project conducted at ICLTT[2] focusing on the creation of a thematic research collection of texts based on the prevalence of sacred literature during the Baroque era, in particular the years from 1650 to 1750. Books of religious instruction and works concerning death and dying were a focal point of Baroque culture. Therefore, the ABaC:us collection holds several texts specific to this genre including sermons, devotional books and works related to the dance-of-death theme. The corpus comprises complete versions, not just samples, of first editions[3] yielding some 165.000 running words. An interdisciplinary approach has been adopted for the creation of this digital corpus, which is designed to meet the needs of both literary/historical and linguistic/lexicographic research.

In order to guarantee easy data-interchange and reusability, the corpus was encoded in TEI (P5).[4] In addition, applied PoS tags and lemma information[5], taken from modern German language, allow for complex search queries and more sophisticated research questions.[6] While starting work on the semantic annotation of the corpus, we saw the need to develop a specific taxonomy, which would also ease the task of semi-automated semantic annotation of the morpho-syntactically annotated corpus and other related texts (Declerck et al., 2011, Mörth et al., 2012). Following a bottom-up strategy, we identified all death-related lexical units such as nom-

---

[1] Partly supported by funds of the Österreichische Nationalbank, Anniversary Fund (project number 14783), the ABaC:us project started in spring 2012. See http://www.oeaw.ac.at/icltt/abacus and http://www.oeaw.ac.at/icltt/abacus-project for more details.

[2] The Institute for Corpus Linguistics and Text Technology (http://www.oeaw.ac.at/icltt/) of the Austrian Academy of Sciences in Vienna pursues corpus-based linguistic and literary research, focusing on the creation and adaptation of corpora and dictionaries as well as technologies for building, accessing and exploiting such data.

[3] The majority of the selected works can be ascribed to the Baroque Catholic writer Abraham a Sancta Clara (1644-1709): e.g. *Mercks Wienn* (1680), *Lösch Wienn* (1680), *Grosse Todten Bruderschafft* (1681), *Augustini Feuriges Hertz* (1693), and *Todten-Capelle* (1710). For detailed information about the author see Eybl (1992) and Knittel (2012).
The ABaC:us collection combines high quality digital texts with image scans of facsimiles of the earliest known prints housed in different libraries such as the Austrian National Library, the Vienna City Library, the Melk Abbey, and the Library of the University of Illinois.

[4] See http://www.tei-c.org/Guidelines/P5/ for details.

[5] PoS tagging has been realized using Tree Tagger, an open standard developed at the University of Stuttgart. See http://www.ims.uni-stuttgart.de/projekte/corplex/TreeTagger/ for more information.

[6] All ABaC:us texts, which represent a non-canonical variety, were tagged using automated tools adapted to the needs of historic language and were afterwards verified by domain-experts.

inal simplicia, compound nouns and multi-word expressions for the personification of death. In addition, all terms and phrases dealing with the "end of life", "dying" and "killing" were identified. In total, more than 1.700 occurrences could be discovered in *Mercks Wienn, Grosse Todten Bruderschafft* and *Todten-Capelle,* the three most important works of our corpus.

The next step consisted in organizing the identified vocabulary in a taxonomy, which is encoded in the SKOS format (Simple Knowledge Organization System)[7]. Based on the Resource Description Framework (RDF)[8], SKOS "provides a model for expressing the basic structure and content of concept schemes such as thesauri, classification schemes, subject heading lists, taxonomies, folksonomies, and other similar types of controlled vocabulary."[9] We chose it because SKOS concepts can be (1) "semantically related to each other in informal hierarchies and association networks", (2) "the SKOS vocabulary itself can be extended to suit the needs of particular communities of practice" and finally, because it (3) "can also be seen as a bridging technology, providing the missing link between the rigorous logical formalism of ontology languages such as OWL and the chaotic, informal and weakly-structured world of Web-based collaboration tools."[10] With the use of SKOS (and RDF), we are also in the position to make our resource compatible with the Linked Data Framework[11].

The following sections provide an overview of the ABaC:us taxonomy and describe the way the language data contained in its labels are linked to web resources in the Linguistic Linked Open Data (LLOD) cloud[12].

2 The ABaC:us Taxonomy

Currently the scheme of the ABaC:us taxonomy consists of 7 concepts comprising 362 terms or phrases, which are encoded in SKOS labels. In addition, 137 compounds and associated terms have been integrated in 4 more temporary concepts, which still await a further processing. The terms included in the labels (both preferred and alternative ones) have been manually excerpted from the original texts and partly normalized. The majority of texts are written in German, some parts in Latin, therefore all lexical labels belong to one of these languages.

Table 1 lists concepts and definitions. Row 3 and 4 show selected examples for preferred and alternative terms in German and Latin—for better readability, a rudimentary English translation has been added. The reader can see how the death as "end of life" (concept/1) and the personalized death (concept/2) are distinguished.

Labels are related to each other by means of the following properties: *abacus:hasTranslation* and inverse *abacus:isTranslationOf,* used for German and corresponding Latin terms, *abacus:hasVariant* and inverse *abacus:isvariantOf* indicate spelling variants.

In order to systemize concept 4 (dealing with "manners of death") we use the annotation property *skos:comment*: "death by accident or circumstances", "death by disease", "death by foreign hand", and "death as a murderer" (i.e. personification of death)[13]. We refrained from creating concepts (labeled *skos:broader*) in this case, as this kind of terms does not represent corpus text. Next, we will link for this purpose to corresponding concepts included in external knowledge sources, allowing thus to distinguish between concepts and terms directly related to our corpus and other knowledge sources that can be used for additional interpretation and classification. This can be seen as the most important difference of the ABaC:us taxonomy to other vocabularies, which are often characterized by strict hierarchical formalisms making them little useful for literary sciences[14].

3 Lexicalization of the Taxonomy

In order to be able to use the taxonomy in the context of NLP applications, there is the need to lexicalize the content of its labels, enriching them with linguistic information. This includes tokenization, lemmatization, PoS tagging, and possibly other levels of natural language (NL) processing. Labels enriched with this information can be better compared to text, which has also been submitted to NL processing tools. If a certain amount of linguistic similarity is found in a text passage with a lexicalized label, this text segment can then be semantically annotated with the concepts the label is associated with.

---

[7] http://www.w3.org/2004/02/skos/
[8] http://www.w3.org/RDF/
[9] http://www.w3.org/TR/2009/NOTE-skos-primer-20090818/
[10] Ibid.
[11] See http://linkeddata.org/
[12] http://linguistics.okfn.org/resources/llod/

[13] Those comments are not displayed in Table 1.
[14] Recently Bradley and Pasin (2012 and 2013) described how informal semantic annotations could become more compatible with computer ontologies and the Semantic Web.

skos:concept	skos:definition	skos:prefLabel	skos:altLabel
concept/1	"Das Ende des Lebens" *"the end of life"*	"Tod" @de "mors" @la *"death"*	"End" "Garauß" "Hintritt" "Todsfall" "Verlust deß Lebens"
concept/2	"Der Tod als Subjekt" *"death as a subject"*	"Tod" @de "mors" @la *"death"*	"dürrer Rippen-Kramer" "General Haut und Bein" "ohngeschliffener Schnitter" "Reuter auf dem fahlen Pferd" "Verbeinter Gesell"
concept/3	"aufhören zu leben" *"the process of dying"*	"sterben" @de "mori" @la *"dying"*	"ad Patres gehen" "das Valete von der Welt nehmen" "dem Tod vnter die Sensen gerathen" "den Todten-Tantz antretten" "in Gott entschlaffen"
concept/4 *(Comment: This concept is about* "Todesarten", *"manners of death")*	"einen bestimmten Tod erleiden" *"specific ways of dying"*	"getötet werden" @de *"to be killed"*	"aufgehängt werden" "erbärmlich hingerichtet werden" "ermort werden" "mit solchen vergifften Pfeil getroffen werden" "zu todt gebissen werden"
concept/5	"Verstorbene, Leichen" *"dead bodies"*	"Toter" @de "mortuus" @la *"corpses"*	"christliche Leiche" "Leichnam" "seelig-verstorbener" "todter Cörper" "Todter"
concept/6	"tot sein" *"to be dead"*	"tot" @de "mortuus" @la *"dead"*	"abgestorben" "der Geist ist hinaus" "leblos" "verblichen" "verstorben"
concept/7	"töten, ermorden" *"to kill someone"*	"töten" @de *"killing"*	"erwürgen" "morden" "todt schlagen" "tödten" "Vergifften"

Table 1: ABaC:us Taxonomy

The model we adopt for the representation of the results of lexicalized labels is the one described by *lemon*[15], developed in the context of the Monnet project[16]. *lemon* is also available as an ontology[17], which has been imported in our taxonomy, so that we can make direct use of all classes and properties of this model.

3.1 Tokenization and Sense Disambiguation

All tokens in ABaC:us have been semi-automatically annotated with lemma and PoS information, following the STTS tag-set (Mörth et al., 2012)[18], so that all parts of the texts selected as relevant terms for inclusion in the labels come already with this information. Thus, our task consists mainly in applying *lemon* ontology elements for annotating the labels of the taxonomy with this linguistic information.

As can be seen in Example **1** below, for the term included in the alternative label "rasender Tod@de" (*raging death*), we make use of the *lemon* property *decomposition* for encoding the results of tokenization. And we use the *lemon* property *altRef,* which has as rdfs:range an entity that is encoded as an instance of the *lemon* class *lexicalSense*[19], for linking to the concept the alternative label is an expression of.

3.2 Linking to external Lexical and Linguistic Resources

We still need to associate the tokens, which are now each encoded as value of the *lemon* property *decomposition*, with morpho-syntactic information. As mentioned earlier, we already have all the information about the corresponding modern German lemmas and PoS (in the STTS format) for all tokens of the corpus.

But, instead of using directly the *lemon* class *lexical entry* and the *lemon* properties *canonical form* and *lexical property* for including the linguistic information we have for every token in the corpus, we are for now linking the values of

[15] *lemon* stands for "Lexicon Model for Ontologies". See http://lemon-model.net/ and McCrae et al. (2012)

[16] See www.monnet-project.eu

[17] See http://www.monnet-project.eu/lemon

[18] The STTS tag-set is described, among others. here: http://www.ims.uni-stuttgart.de/forschung/ressourcen/lexika/TagSets/stts-table.html

[19] See http://lemon-model.net/lemon.rdf for the whole list of properties and classes of *lemon.*

the *lemon* property *decomposition* to already existing lexical entries that are encoded in the LOD format. We choose for this the actual DBpedia instantiation of Wiktionary[20]. There we get also the information that “rasender” is an adjective with lemma “rasend” and that “Tod” is a noun with lemma “Tod” (see Example **1** below)[21]. The two meanings we have distinguished in the ABaC:us taxonomy for “Tod” (*death*), as the “end of life” and as “a subject”, are also present in this external resource[22]. Depending on the specific Wiktionary entries, we have a variable number of sense-specific translations at our disposal. The word “Tod”, with the meaning “end of life”, is provided with 44 translations. We can automatically add those labels to our taxonomy and link them to the German labels via the *abacus:isTranslationOf* property, and so support cross-lingual access to our semantically annotated corpus. It was more difficult to find an English equivalent for the second meaning of “death”, “death as a subject”[23], since no direct translation for English is given in this instantiation of Wiktionary. The same can be said of the ambiguous German lemma “rasend” (*raging*).

As a result, the term “rasender Tod@de” (*raging death*) is now encoded in our taxonomy (with *lemon* being integrated) this way:

```
<http://www.oeaw.ac.at/icltt/abacus/term/2.004-de>
rdf:type owl:NamedIndividual , skosxl:Label ;
skosxl:literalForm "rasender Tod"@de ;
<http://www.monnet-
project.eu/lemon#decomposition>
<http://wiktionary.dbpedia.org/page/rasend-German-
Adjective-1de> ;
<http://www.monnet-
project.eu/lemon#decomposition>
<http://wiktionary.dbpedia.org/page/Tod-German-
Noun-2de> ;
<http://www.lemon-model.net/lemon#altRef>
<http://www.oeaw.ac.at/icltt/abacus/concept/2> ;
abacus:isVariantOf
<http://www.oeaw.ac.at/icltt/abacus/term/2.003-de> .
```

Example 1: The simplified entry for the label “rasender Tod” (*raging death*)

[20] See http://dbpedia.org/Wiktionary. There, *lemon* is also used for the description of certain lexical properties.

[21] But in the longer term we will use the *lemon* constructs for linking to the URIs associated to those pieces of information in the DBpedia coverage of Wiktionary.

[22] See wiktionary.dbpedia.org/page/Tod-German-Noun-1de and wiktionary.dbpedia.org/page/Tod-German-Noun-2de for abacus:concept/1 and abacus:concept/2 respectively.

[23] http://wiktionary.dbpedia.org/page/death-English-Noun-2en.

4 Conclusion

The ABaC:us collection contains a wide range of death-related linguistic vocabulary deriving from the Baroque era. Its writers were extremely inventive in paraphrasing experiences with death and dying. Thus, one integral approach was to make those different concepts more easily discernible. The numerous SKOS labels in the ABaC:us taxonomy give evidence of how the culture of death and dying was transmitted in lexical and linguistic patterns. By making those patterns accessible and reusable on the (L)LOD, we complement existing contemporary concepts of the topic and provide a basis for sharing and comparing the concepts, which can be used in NLP applications in the context of eHumanities.

References

John Bradley, Michele Pasin. 2012. Annotation and Ontology in most Humanities research: accommodating a more informal interpretation context. DH2012 NeDiMaH Ontology Workshop.

John Bradley, Michele Pasin. 2013. Fitting Personal Interpretations with the Semantic Web. In: *Proceedings of Digital Humanities 2013.* University of Nebraska-Lincoln:118-120.

Thierry Declerck, Ulrike Czeitschner, Karlheinz Mörth, Claudia Resch, Gerhard Budin. 2011. A Text Technology Infrastructure for Annotating Corpora in the eHumanities. In: *Proceedings of the International Conference on Theory and Practice of Digital Libraries* (TPDL-2011):457-460.

Franz M. Eybl. 1992. Abraham a Sancta Clara. Vom Prediger zum Schriftsteller. Max Niemeyer, Tübingen, D.

Anton Philipp Knittel (Ed.). 2012. Unterhaltender Prediger und gelehrter Stofflieferant. Abraham a Sancta Clara (1644-1709). Beiträge eines Symposions anlässlich seines 300. Todestages. Edition Isele, Eggingen, D.

John McCrae, Guadalupe Aguado-de-Cea, Paul Buitelaar, Philipp Cimiano, Thierry Declerck, Asunción Gómez-Pérez, Jorge Gracia, Laura Hollink, Elena Montiel-Ponsoda, Dennis Spohr, Tobias Wunner. 2012. Interchanging lexical resources on the Semantic Web. In: *Language Resources and Evaluation.* Vol. 46, Issue 4, Springer:701-719.

Karlheinz Mörth, Claudia Resch, Thierry Declerck, Ulrike Czeitschner. 2012. Linguistic and Semantic Annotation in Religious Memento Mori Literature. In: *Proceedings of the LREC'2012 Workshop: Language Resources and Evaluation for Religious Texts (LRE-Rel-12).* ELRA: 49-52.

Towards a System for Dynamic Language Resources in LOD

Kiril Simov
Linguistic Modelling Department
IICT-BAS, Sofia, Bulgaria
kivs@bultreebank.org

Abstract

Formalization and representation of the language resources life cycle in a formal language to support the creation, update and application of the language resource instances is made possible via the developments in the area of ontologies and Linked Open Data. In the paper we present some of the basic functionalities of a system to support dynamic language resources.

1 Introduction

Recent developments in Natural Language Processing (NLP) are heading towards knowledge rich resources and technology. Integration of linguistically sound grammars, sophisticated machine learning settings and world knowledge background is possible given the availability of the appropriate resources: deep multilingual treebanks, which represent detailed syntactic and semantic information. Such knowledge is mainly present in deeply processed language resources like HPSG-based (LFG-based) treebanks (RedWoods treebank, DeepBank, and others). The inherent characteristics of these language resources is their dynamic nature. They are constructed simultaneously with the development of a deep grammar in the corresponding linguistic formalism. The grammar is used to produce all potential analyses of the sentences within the treebank. The correct analyses are selected manually on the base of linguistic discriminators which would determine the correct linguistic production. The annotation process of the sentences provides feedback for the grammar writer to update the grammar. The life cycle of a dynamic language resource can be naturally supported by the semantic technology behind the ontology and LOD - modeling the grammatical knowledge as well as the annotation knowledge; supporting the annotation process; reclassification after changes within the grammar; querying the available resources; exploitation in real applications. The addition of a LOD component to the system would facilitate the exchange of language resources created in this way and would support the access to the existing resources on the web.

The structure of this paper is as follows: next section introduces related work; Section 3 discusses the main requirements of Knowledge-based Language Resources; Section 4 presents dynamic treebanking as an example of a Knowledge-based Language Resource; Section 5 concludes the paper.

2 Related work

Linked Open Data has been in active development during the last decade. (Bizer et al., 2009) defines the principles for publishing RDF data on the Web:

- Use URIs as (unique) names for things,
- Use HTTP URIs so that people can look up those names,
- When someone looks up a URI, provide useful information, using Web standards such as RDF, and SPARQL,
- Include links to other URIs, so that they can discover more things.

Usually LOD is grouped in datasets, equipped with ontology. Examples of LOD Datasets are: (1) **DBPedia.** DBPedia dataset is based on extraction of structural information from Wikipedia, which is presented in RDF form; (2) **Freebase.** Freebase is a community-curated database of well-known people, places, and things; (3) **Geonames.** A geographical database. The different LOD datasets are interlinked via owl:sameAs statements which state that some individuals (represented via different URIs) denote the same object in the world.

The ontologies in LOD define the conceptualization of the world and provide mechanism for inference, search and maintenance over the data within the datasets. Thus ontologies are a powerful mechanism for representation and manipulation of knowledge. They can be used to define different views over the same information and facilitate inference for consistency checking. Unfortunately, the conceptualization encoded in ontologies could follow different ontological assumptions. Thus, when someone uses datasets from LOD, he/she has to pay attention to the way in which they are conceptualized. One solution for the diversity of the ontologies within LOD is the definition of a common unifying ontology.

Different communities have already defined and published their datasets on the LOD cloud. In the last years the linguistic community also moved towards the creation of Linguistic Linked Open Data (LLOD). The area has been under active development. Many of the community activities are reported here:

- The Open Linguistics Working Group: http://linguistics.okfn.org
- W3C Ontology-Lexica Community Group: http://www.w3.org/community/ontolex

(Chiarcos et al., 2012) list the following advantages:

- Representation and modeling
- Structural interoperability
- Federation
- Ecosystem
- Expressivity
- Conceptual interoperability
- Dynamic import

In this paper we rely on several of these advantages. More specifically, on the representation and modeling of language resources and their dynamic nature.

As an example of a knowledge-based language resource (KBLR) we follow the methodology for dynamic treebanking as it was implemented within the Redwood, DeepBank (Flickinger et al., 2012), BulTreeBank (Simov et al., 2004) treebanks and the infrastructure for dynamic treebanking INESS (Rosén et al., 2012). For example, the Redwoods treebank was compiled by coupling English Resource Grammar (ERG) and a tree selection module of [incr tsdb()] (see (Oepen, 1999) and (Oepen et al., 2002)). ERG produces very detailed syntacto-semantic analyses of the input sentence. For many sentences, HPSG processor (e.g. LKB — (Copestake, 2002)) overgenerates, producing analyses that are not acceptable. From the complete analyses different components can be extracted in order to highlight different views over the analyses: (1) derivation trees composed of identifiers of lexical items and constructions used to build the analysis; (2) phrase structure trees; and (3) underspecified MRS representations. From these types of information the most important with respect to the treebank construction is the first one, because it is good enough to support the reconstruction of the HPSG analysis by a parser. The steps of constructing the Redwood treebank are:

- LKB produces all possible analyses according to the current version of ERG;
- The tree comparison module provides a mechanism for selection of the correct analyses;
- The selection is done via basic properties (called also discriminating properties) which discriminate between the different analyses;
- The set of the selected basic properties are stored in the treebank database for later use in case of a treebank update.
- The update of the grammar initiates an update of the treebank itself. All the sentences that were annotated on the basis of the previous version of the grammar are analyzed again. The selection is done on the basis of the previous annotator selections.

We aim at designing and implementing a system that supports the creation and maintenance of language resources following the ideas of dynamic treebanking.

3 Knowledge-Based Language Resources

Our goal is to implement a system for supporting the whole life cycle of the creation and usage of language resources at knowledge level. This process includes formal modeling of different aspects of the LRs management, such as:

- Representation of the annotation schema (e.g. a grammar). Here we envisage a representation of linguistic ontology, defining the vocabulary for describing linguistic objects and their basic properties, and constraints determining the actual linguistic objects.

- Representation of the annotation (analyses with respect to the annotation schema). We expect the annotation to be a representation of linguistic objects. Additionally, we require the implementation of appropriate tools for supporting creation of the annotation (automatically and/or manually). Checking consistency of annotation. Searching in the knowledge base.

- Creation (management) of language resources. Here we expect all the metainformation to be modeled and stored in the process of creation and evolution of LRs. Also, some of the activities in the process of creation and management of LRs to be supported on knowledge level.

- Usage of language resources. Originally each LR is created with a task in mind, but frequently this LR is used for many other tasks. In these cases usually the language resource is adapted to the new task including reformulation of the knowledge, stored in the LR, extensions with information from other resources and human intervention. Thus LR are directly connected to the actual usage. We view the knowledge-based approach to language resources management as being ideal to support all these requirements.

Modeling the annotation schema and annotations using ontologies is motivated by the need of complex and detailed language resources. Such language resources cannot be theory independent because of the following reasons:

- For real applications - detailed analyses are needed. The corresponding language resources need to incorporate the same level of granularity as the analyses necessary for the applications.

- On a certain level of granularity the annotation scheme becomes very complicated to be processed manually in a consistent way. Thus, a certain formalization will be necessary.

- On a certain level of granularity some linguistic theory has to be exploited. When it is possible, it is better to select existing theories instead of inventing a new "annotation" theory.

The example presented in the next section is based on the Head-driven Phrase Structure Grammar (HPSG). There are several reasons for this choice. HPSG is already formalized and this formalization allows a conversion between different formalisms. There exist examples of dynamic language resources created within this linguistic theory. The created framework could be easily ported to the setup of the knowledge-based language resources.

4 Dynamic Treebanking

This section is heavily based on (Simov, 2003). As it was stated above, we aim at modeling the HPSG dynamic treebanking as a knowledge-based language resource. First, we need to formalize the HPSG Language Model. It includes the following components:

- Linguistic objects in HPSG are represented as directed graphs called feature structures. The analyses of sentences are represented as complete feature structures in which all the constraints stated in the sort hierarchy and the grammar are satisfied.

- Sort hierarchy[1] defines a linguistic ontology. It represents the types of linguistic objects and their characteristics (features). The sort hierarchy determines the possible linguistic objects.

- Grammar is represented as a theory within a logical formalism over the sort hierarchy. It constraints the possible linguistic objects to the actual linguistic objects. The grammar is divided in two parts: (1) HPSG Universal and Language[2] Specific Principles; and (2) Language Specific Lexicon. Each principle and

[1]Sometimes it is called type hierarchy.

[2]English, Bulgarian, Tagalog or another natural language

each lexical entry is represented as a formula in the logical formalism. The formulas include sort assignment, equality of compositions of features as elementary formulas and full logical set of connectives over the elementary formulas.[3]

In order to support the HPSG dynamic treebank as knowledge-based language resources management we have to be able to support at least the following tasks:

- Implementation of an Annotation Schema. The sort hierarchy can be represented as an ontology in a straightforward way. The representation of formulas from the grammar is possible, but the standard inference for OWL DL can not be used, because OWL DL does not support equality.
- Analyses of sentences are represented as a set of complete instances. Without appropriate inference over the annotation schema we rely on an external processor which produces all the acceptable analyses over the grammar. These analyses are translated as RDF graphs using the ontology behind the annotation schema.
- Minimisation of manual work for the creation of the treebank. We select the correct analysis from the set of all analyses via classification of elementary formulas with respect to these analyses. After finite number of steps the correct analysis is selected. The process is described below.
- Adaptation of the treebank to different uses. Some usages require different views over the data. This is implemented by defining a new ontology for each new view over the treebank. See below.
- Dynamic nature is supported by a re-design of the annotation schema and re-classification of the existing analyses with respect to the new annotation schema. See below.

Corpus Annotation. As it is stated above, the corpus annotation within this framework is based on parse selection from a number of automatically constructed sentence parses. There are tree steps in the annotation process: (1) Pre-processing of the selected sentence. This step includes a segmentation of the text in sentences. Each sentence is annotated morphologically. (2) The result is encoded as a partial feature graph and it is further processed by an HPSG processor to a set of complete feature graphs. (3) The parse selection is considered as a classification with respect to the result from the previous step based on partial descriptions provided by the annotator.

Classification is done by means of index over the set of the produced parses. First, the intersection of all graphs is calculated. We assume that this part is true. Then an index is created on the basis of the elementary formulas within the graph. The index is a decision tree over the analyses. Each node in the tree is marked with an elementary formula which can be true or false. After selection of the correct value the corresponding edge is traversed to the next node. In this way the number of possible choices is reduced. The leaves of the tree are marked with the parses. Thus, in the index the formulas are chosen in such a way that each path from the root of the tree to some of its leaves determines exactly one graph in the initial set of graphs.

In the annotation the annotator supplies partial formulas (elementary formulas) about the true analysis. The index is traversed and the number of the possible choices is reduced. The process is repeated to the moment when only one analysis is selected. This analysis is stored within the treebank.

There is a problem with this annotation procedure. Any index represents just one view on the classification over the set of graphs. The annotator can have different views of classification over the same set of graphs. This means that at some moment the annotator could be not able to provide a formula that is in the index.

This clash between a predetermined way of classification scheme and the linguistic intuition could be resolved by construction by all the indices. In this case, the annotator chooses the most appropriate for him/her type of classification. These indices are represented as a forest in order to minimize the size of the representation. The annotation process proceeds according to the following classification algorithm:

1. The nodes in the index are available to be

[3]We will not be more specific here about the logical language and the interpretation of the language. Interested reader can consult the appropriate literature.

chosen by the annotator

2. The annotator decides on an elementary formula about the sentence
3. The elementary formula is found in the index and the number of the possible graphs is reduced
4. If there is only one possible graph, it is returned as a result, otherwise the algorithm returns to step 2

The number of the selections are in the worst case equal to the number of all analyses for the sentence. This can happen when the annotator rules out exactly one analysis per choice. The average number of selections is a logarithm from the number of the analyses. An important advantage of this selection-analysis-approach is that the annotator works locally. Thus, the number of parameters necessary to be considered simultaneously is minimized.

Corpus Update. If at some step of annotation the annotator cannot select any elementary formula from the index, we assume that there is no correct analysis in the set for the sentence. This fact is reported back to the grammar writer in order to modify the grammar. In such cases of grammar update the annotated sentences in the treebank needs to be reclassified with respect to the new annotation schema. The change of the annotation schema could be necessary in many cases like:

- Modifications in the target linguistic model of the elements in the corpus,
- New developments in the linguistic theory,
- Misleading decisions, taken during the design phase of the corpus development,
- New applications, for which the corpus might be adjusted.

In each of these cases the result is a new annotation schema. The treebank created with respect to the previous annotation schema could not be valid anymore with respect to the new one. The main question in this case is: How to use the existing corpus in the new circumstances and at minimal costs? In the case of knowledge-based language resources the idea of reclassification could be implemented as a transfer of all the relevant knowledge represented from the old annotation scheme to the new one. The transfer of the linguistic knowledge is defined by correspondence rules of the following format $\delta_{old} \Rightarrow \delta_{new}$, where δ_{old} is a formula with respect to the old annotation schema and δ_{new} is a corresponding formula with respect to the new annotation schema. In most cases the transfer rules are for formulas that are the same with respect to both annotation schemas. In such settings the reclassification algorithm for an HPSG treebank is as follows:

- For a sentence in the treebank we construct a new set of complete graphs $\{G_1, \ldots, G_n\}$,
- From the existing annotation we construct a set $EDnew$ of formulas using the correspondence rules,
- The set $EDnew$ is used for a classification of the sentences with respect to the set $\{G_1, \ldots, G_n\}$.

There could be the case when the transferred knowledge is not enough to classify the sentence with respect to the new set of graphs. In such a case manual intervention of an annotator will be necessary in order to complete the annotation.

Corpus Usage. Reclassification can be exploited in cases when the treebank will be used for a particular task which requires a different view over the represented linguistic knowledge. For example, for evaluation of parsers usually one needs to convert the treebank into a format comparable to the format of the parses. In case of knowledge-based language resources such evaluation could be done via representation of the parses with respect to annotation schema with the KBLR system. Then we apply appropriate reclassification of both: the treebank and the parses. Defining different annotation schema for the evaluation schema allows us to measure the performance of the parser with respect to different phenomena when this is necessary. For example, most of the parsers will be good on non-recursive phrases, but they will make mistakes over phenomena like PP attachment, coordination, etc. Thus, we could design annotation schema that hides the easy cases and compare the parses and the treebank on the hard problems.

Documentation of Annotation Process. Formalization of the annotation process via ontologies and knowledge bases of instances provide a rich mechanism for storing important information from the process of the annotation. For this we envisage the usage of the so called annotation context ontology. This ontology describes the annotation setup: annotation schema, version of the HPSG grammar, annotators, time information, different annotation tasks. Each time some annotation action is performed appropriate record is created and stored. This will allow very detailed description of the annotation process. For example, it will allow to search for all the sentences annotated by some annotator, even after several modifications of the annotation schema and the eventual reclassification of the data.

Also such recording will help further usage of the treebank. For example, each usage could be reported with respect to the annotation context ontology. Later when somebody wants to use the treebank for evaluation of a new parser he/she could first examine the setups in which the treebank was used for similar tasks and then design a new one. Similarly the history of the annotation process could be useful in the process of design and implementation of new language resources.

Created in such a way language resources provide an easy connection to linked open data. Each knowledge-based language resource can be seen as a LOD dataset in which:

- The annotation schema is represented as an ontology,
- The annotated corpus is a set of instance data,
- The actual representation of the ontology and instance data in RDF is a trivial task,
- The documentation can be generated from the documentation of the annotation schema and published as a set of web pages dynamically,
- The description of the annotation process is also part of the dataset.

Integration with LOD is possible in both directions: (1) Any version of the created language resource could be immediately made available as a LOD dataset. This would facilitate the further use of the resource and feedback response as early as possible. (2) In some cases access the annotation process could gain from the access to other knowledge-based language resources. This can be done via inference mechanisms like classification and reclassification described above.

5 Conclusion and Future Work

This paper presented the main requirements for the creation of knowledge-based language resources on the basis of HPSG treebanking. As it is presented here, the actual implementation depends heavily on external processors like LKB system for producing HPSG analyses of sentences. In future, a system supporting knowledge-based language resources management will need integration with many external systems. But in our view, for such a system to be widely used, it needs to provide also internal tools working directly with ontologies and instance data. These tools need to support the complete manual annotation cycle, not just the selection of correct analysis. The cycle would include also: creation of processing procedure directly over RDF graphs like regular grammars, rules, transformation scripts, etc. These services will include many standard tools that already exist in the world of Linked Open Data. But there are also needs for new specific tools which are specially designed for the creation and management of KBLR. Another group of tools necessary to be implemented are: visualization and editing facilities.

In many respects we will follow the design and the implementation of CLaRK system — (Simov et al., 2003). In this context we consider RDF graphs corresponding to XML documents, ontologies corresponding to DTDs or XML schemas, etc. We believe that this is the way in which exploitation of language resources and technologies will be made widely used. Such a system is especially important within initiatives like CLARIN[4] whose huge target group of end users would like to exploit the available language resources and tools for their specific tasks. Many of them are not familiar with the principles behind the language resources and technologies. Knowledge-based system are perfect to support such kind of users. Especially important for them is the annotation context ontology which will provide them with access to the best practises in usage of language technologies. We envisage developing our system in this direction within the Bulgarian part of CLARIN infrastructure. We envisage extension of the annotation context ontology to incorporate also information about creation of language technologies and their dependency on language resources.

[4] www.clarin.eu

Acknowledgments

The work reported here is partially supported by the FP7 Capacity Project AComIn: Advanced Computing for Innovation (316087). I would like to thank Petya Osenova for many discussions on the topics reported in the paper and also for comments on early version of the paper. I am also grateful to colleagues from Ontotext AD who I have been working with on some aspects of LOD in the last years.

References

Christian Bizer, Tom Heath, and Tim Berners-Lee. 2009. Linked data-the story so far. *International Journal on Semantic Web and Information Systems (IJSWIS)*, 5(3):1–22.

Christian Chiarcos, John McCrae, Philipp Cimiano, and Christiane Fellbaum, 2012. *Towards open data for linguistics: Lexical Linked Data.*

Ann Copestake. 2002. *Implementing Typed Feature Structure Grammars*. CSLI lecture notes: Center for the Study of Language and Information. CTR FOR STUDY OF LANG & INFO.

Daniel Flickinger, Yi Zhang, and Valia Kordoni. 2012. Deepbank: A dynamically annotated treebank of the wall street journal. In *Proceedings of the Eleventh International Workshop on Treebanks and Linguistic Theories*, pages 85–96. Edições Colibri.

Stephan Oepen, Kristina Toutanova, Stuart Shieber, Christopher Manning, Dan Flickinger, and Thorsten Brants. 2002. The lingo redwoods treebank motivation and preliminary applications. In *Proceedings of the 19th international conference on Computational linguistics - Volume 2*, COLING '02, pages 1–5, Stroudsburg, PA, USA. Association for Computational Linguistics.

Stephan Oepen. 1999. *[incr tsdb()] - Competence and Performance Laboratory.* Saarland University.

Victoria Rosén, Paul Meurer, Gyri Smrdal Losnegaard, Gunn Inger Lyse, Koenraad De Smedt, Martha Thunes, and Helge Dyvik. 2012. An integrated web-based treebank annotation system. In *Proceedings of the Eleventh International Workshop on Treebanks and Linguistic Theories*, pages 157–167. Edições Colibri.

Kiril Ivanov Simov, Alexander Simov, Milen Kouylekov, Krasimira Ivanova, Ilko Grigorov, and Hristo Ganev. 2003. Development of corpora within the CLaRK system: The BulTreeBank project experience. In *Proceedings of the 10th conference of the European chapter of the Association for Computational Linguistics*, EACL '03, pages 243–246, Budapest, Hungary.

Kiril Simov, Petya Osenova, Alexander Simov, and Milen Kouylekov. 2004. Design and implementation of the Bulgarian HPSG-based treebank. In *Journal of Research on Language and Computation, Special Issue*, pages 495–522, Kluwer Academic Publishers.

Kiril Ivanov Simov. 2003. Hpsg-based annotation scheme for corpora development and parsing evaluation. In Nicolas Nicolov, Kalina Bontcheva, Galia Angelova, and Ruslan Mitkov, editors, *RANLP*, volume 260 of *Current Issues in Linguistic Theory (CILT)*, pages 327–336. John Benjamins, Amsterdam/Philadelphia.

Applications of Semantic Publishing

Borislav Popov
Ontotext AD
borislav.popov@ontotext.com

1 Abstract

In recent years Semantic publishing applications get more and more domain-spread and user-oriented in several aspects, among which: customization and re-purpose of data and content reflecting the user needs in various domains; focused summaries with respect to user interests; high relevance of the retrieved information and minimal effort in receiving it.

There are various works, exploring the relation between publishing and Linked Open Data, since the latter enriches the semantics successfully across various domains. In (Villazon-Terrazas et. al 2012), for example, authors present their idea on a life cycle model (specification, modeling, generation, linking, publication, exploitation) and demonstrate its application within various domains. At the same time, in (Mendes et. al 2011) a DBpedia service has been presented (called DBpedia Spotlight), which automatically annotates text documents with DBpedia URI's using the DBpedia in-house ontology. Similarly, Zemanta[1] provides a plug-in to content creators, which recommends links to relevant content (articles, keywords, tags). Our approach is generally in-line with these ideas and services – domain specific applications, automatic semantic annotation, and addition of relevant linked content. However, our focus is preferably on: the trade-off between the semantic knowledge holders (ontologies, linked data) and their language reflection (domain texts), mediated by the linguistic processing pipelines; the adaptive flexibility of the constructed applications and the efficient storage and publishing of large data.

Within Ontotext, examples of mass media, semantic publishing web sites, such as the BBC's sport web[2] and the official web of the London's Olympics 2013, have proven to attract a multi-million user bases. Behind such applications, as revealed by lead engineers at the BBC[3], there lies the complex architecture of the state-of-the-art Semantic and Text Analytics technologies, such as in-house: fast RDF database management system OWLIM[4] and knowledge management platforms KIM[5]; for robust semantic annotation and search, as well as for text analytics applications.

Both platforms are incorporated into numerous successful Semantic Publishing Solutions (including the BBC Sport[6], Press Association[7], Newz[8], EuroMoney[9], Publicis[10] etc.). For the core methodology see (Kiryakov et. al 2003) and (Popov et. al 2003). Starting with the FIFA 2010 BBC web site, through the London Olympics, feeding the official news site with enriched content together with Press Association, we have built domain expertise, sound solution implementation methodologies, and a semantic publishing platform to serve our clients. Beyond mass media, specialized publishers licensed our products and commissioned us for customizations - like Euromoney for macroeconomic report analytics and Oxford University Press and IET for high value scientific content.

This talk aims to describe the parameters of our domain adaptation approach, used successfully in many projects for more than 5 years, to build rigorous semantic publishing solutions.

Our strategy relies on the calibration between the RDF semantic repository OWLIM, the semantic resources in KIM and the optimized Text Analytics techniques including methodologies for fast creation of gold data in the selected do-

---

1 http://en.wikipedia.org/wiki/Zemanta
2 www.bbc.com/sport
3 www.bbc.co.uk/blogs/bbcinternet/2012/04/sports_dynamic_semantic.html
4 www.ontotext.com/owlim
5 http://www.ontotext.com/kim
6 http://www.ontotext.com/publishing
7 http://www.pressassociation.com/
8 newz.nl
9 http://www.euromoney.com/
10 http://www.publicis.de/

main; focused curation of the automatically analyzed data and the application of advanced machine learning algorithms in data clustering. Thus, the success of our solutions lays in the customization of the advanced semantic technologies in combination with text analytics techniques, tuned to the needs of publishers and adapted to the requested domains.

2 Short Bio

Borislav Popov is the Head of the Semantic Annotation and Search division at Ontotext. He has specialized in AI, spent some time on landmark projects in the financial and ERP industry across the Balkans with clients like BASF and AC Nielsen. He is a part of Ontotext since its founding and leads the company's involvement in several EC funded projects with multi–million budgets. He took part in the birth of the KIM Platform and since then is leading both its development, the semantic annotation and search division and is primarily responsible for all the solution the group provides. Under his guidance the group delivered multiple solutions in Publishing and Media for the BBC, Press Association and several other major customers.

References

Atanas Kiryakov, Borislav Popov, Damyan Ognyanoff, Dimitar Manov, Angel Kirilov, Miroslav Goranov. 2003. Semantic Annotation, Indexing, and Retrieval. In: *2nd International Semantic Web Conference (ISWC2003)*, 20-23 October 2003, Florida, USA. LNAI Vol. 2870, pp. 484-499, Springer-Verlag Berlin Heidelberg 2003.

Pablo N. Mendes, Max Jakob, Andres Garcia-Silva and Christian Bizer. 2011. DBpedia spotlight: shedding light on the web of documents. In: *Proceedings of the 7th International Conference on Semantic Systems*, pp. 1-8, ACM, New York, NY, USA.

Borislav Popov, Atanas Kiryakov, Angel Kirilov, Dimitar Manov, Damyan Ognyanoff and Miroslav Goranov. 2003. KIM – Semantic Annotation Platform. In: *2nd International Semantic Web Conference (ISWC2003)*, 20-23 October 2003, Florida, USA. LNAI Vol. 2870, pp. 834-849, Springer-Verlag Berlin Heidelberg 2003.

Boris Villazon-Terrazas, Daniel Vila-Suero, Daniel Garijo, Luis M. Vilches-Blazquez, Maria Poveda-Villalon, Jose Mora, Oscar Corcho, and Asuncion Gomez-Perez. 2012. Publishing Linked Data - There is no One-Size-Fits-All Formula. In: *Proceedings of the European Data Forum 2012, Copenague, Dinamarca.*

Literature-driven Curation for Taxonomic Name Databases

Hui Yang, Alistair Willis, David R. Morse, Anne de Roeck
Department of Computing and Communications
{Hui.Yang, Alistair.Willis, David.Morse,
Anne.deRoeck}@open.ac.uk

Abstract

Digitized biodiversity literature provides a wealth of content for using biodiversity knowledge by machines. However, identifying taxonomic names and the associated semantic metadata is a difficult and labour intensive process. We present a system to support human assisted creation of semantic metadata. Information extraction techniques automatically identify taxonomic names from scanned documents. They are then presented to users for manual correction or verification. The tools that support the curation process include taxonomic name identification and mapping, and community-driven taxonomic name verification. Our research shows the potential for these information extraction techniques to support research and curation in disciplines dependent upon scanned documents.

1 Introduction

Our understanding of the natural world is rapidly increasing. At the same time, issues in biodiversity are shown to be relevant to many important policy areas, such as climate change, food security and habitat management. Biological taxonomy is a discipline that underlies all of these areas; understanding species, their behaviours and how they interact is of critical importance in being able to manage commercially important land and environment use (SCBD, 2008).

A major difficulty facing the curation of comprehensive taxonomic databases is incorporating the knowledge that is currently contained only in the printed literature, which spans well over one hundred million pages. Much of the literature, especially old taxonomic monographs that are both rare documents and extremely valuable for taxonomic research, are almost entirely in paper-print form and are not directly accessible electronically. Recent large-scale digitization projects like the Biodiversity Heritage Library [1] (BHL) have worked to digitize the (out of copyright) biodiversity literature held in natural history museums and other libraries' collections. However, due to the lack of semantic metadata, the tasks of finding, extracting, and managing the knowledge contained in these volumes is still a primarily manual process and remains extremely difficult and labour-intensive. The difficulty in accessing the existing taxonomic literature is a severe impediment to research and delivery of the subject's benefits (Godfray, 2002). Semantic tagging of organism mentions in biodiversity literature has recently been regarded as a pivotal step to facilitate taxonomy-aware text mining applications, including species-specific document retrieval (Sarka, 2007), linking biodiversity databases (White, 2007), and semantic enrichment of biodiversity articles (Penev et al, 2010).

Semantic web is a potential solution to the problems of data fragmentation and knowledge management if the appropriate metadata can be created (Page, 2006). However, manually creating this metadata is an enormous and unrealistic task. The verification process of checking the validity of a taxonomic name is a specialist task requiring expert skills.

In this paper, we present a semi-automated system that aims to develop a literature-driven curation process among practicing taxonomists, by providing tools to help taxonomists identify and validate appropriate taxonomic names from the scanned historical literature. Potential taxonomic names are automatically extracted from scanned biodiversity documents with their associated contextual information. These are presented for validation to taxonomic curators via an online web service. The manually verified or corrected names can then be indexed, and the semantic data stored, using the Darwin Core biodiversity data standard.

2 System Framework

Figure 1 shows the process for obtaining metadata and curating taxonomic names. Publishers who specialise in biological taxonomy often add appropriate metadata (Penev et al. 2010), but for scanned literature, this is generally not available.

[1] http://www.biodiversitylibrary.org

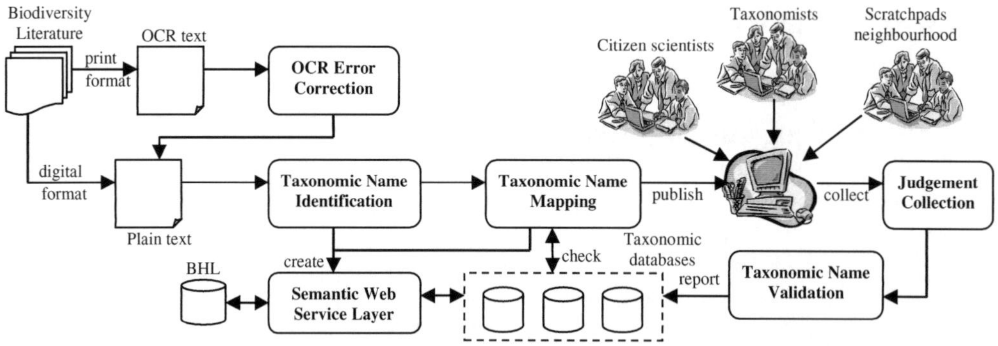

Figure 1. System framework of literature-driven curation for taxonomic databases

The image files from scanned literature are processed through the ABBY FineReader or PrimeReader Optical Character Recognition (OCR) software to generate a plain text file.

Next, we identify those tokens in the plain text that may be taxonomic names (possibly containing errors through imperfect OCR, or other transcription errors). We use an information extraction tool for Named Entity Recognition (NER) based on Conditional Random Fields (CRFs) (Lafferty et al., 2001). The detected names are then mapped onto unique identifiers across a range of taxonomic databases such as uBio Name Bank[2], Encyclopaedia of Life (EoL)[3], and Catalogue of Life (CoL)[4].

Taxonomic names that cannot be found in online databases will be validated manually. Potential unknown taxonomic names are presented for validation or correction to the research community via the Scratchpads social network[5] (e.g., professional taxonomists, experienced citizen scientists and other biodiversity specialists) in a community-driven verification process. The newly verified taxonomic name, along with additional metadata recording the user who verified the name, its context and bibliographic details is published as a semantic web service layer (currently a Scratchpads portal).

3 Taxonomic Name Recognition

Automatic identification of taxonomic names from biodiversity text has attracted increasing research interest over the past few years, but is difficult because of the problems of erroneous transcription and synonymy. There may be orthographic and other term variation in names assigned to the same species (Remsen, 2011). For example, *Actinobacillus actionomy*, *Actinobacillus actionomyce*, and *Actinobacillus actionomycetam* could all be variants of the same name. In addition, scanned documents can cause many OCR errors due to outdated fonts, complex terms, and aspects such as blemishes and stains on the scanned pages. Wei et al (2010) have observed that 35% of taxonomic names in scanned documents contain an error, and this creates difficulties for term recognition (Willis et al. 2009). For example, erroneous OCR might propose '*o*' in place of '*c*' for the taxon *Pioa*, not a known name, rather than *Pica* (European magpie).

Approaches to taxonomic name recognition (TNR) span a broad range from traditional dictionary lookup (Gerner et al., 2010; Koning et al., 2005; Leary et al., 2007) combined with linguistic rule-based (Sautter et al., 2006) to pure machine learning (Akella et al., 2012).

In our system (Figure 1), the first stage is identifying potential taxonomic names. We used a supervised learning algorithm implemented by the CRF++ Package[6]. Compared to other machine learning algorithms, CRFs are good at sequence segmentation labeling tasks such as Named Entity Recognition, which have been shown to be effective for biological entity identification in the biomedical literature (Yang et al. 2008). They can be easily adapted to similar tasks like Taxonomic Name Recognition (TNR).

3.1 Dataset Preparation and Annotation

To assess the performance of the CRFs on taxonomic texts, we generated training and test sets from scanned volumes between 1879 and 1911 from the Biodiversity Heritage Library (BHL).

Annotations were carried out using the BRAT Rapid Annotation Tool (BRAT)[7] (Stenetorp et

---

[2] http://www.ubio.org/

[3] http://eol.org/

[4] http://www.catalogueoflife.org/

[5] http://scratchpads.eu

[6] http://crfpp.googlecode.com/svn/trunk/doc/index.html

[7] http://brat.nlplab.org/

al., 2012) to mark up taxonomic elements in biodiversity literature. All mentions of taxonomic names in the text were manually tagged and linked to identifiers in external taxonomic databases (i.e. uBio Name Bank, Catalogue of Life, and Encyclopaedia of Life) where possible. Annotated mentions were also assigned to several categories that indicate specific linguistic or semantic features (e.g. taxonomic rank, genus abbreviation or omission) for evaluation analysis. The manually annotated dataset consists of:

(a) **Training data.** We selected three BHL volumes of different animal groups: *Coleoptera* (Beetles)[8], *Aves* (Birds)[9], and *Pisces* (Fish)[10] as the training data to build a CRF-based taxon recogniser. The volume text used for the annotation is *clear text*, i.e. text from which OCR errors are removed, which was obtained from the INOTAXA Project[11]. Table 1 reports the statistical annotation information about these three volumes.

	#Pages	**#Taxonomic Names**
Coleoptera	324	7,264
Aves	553	8,354
Pisces	234	4,915

Table 1. The statistics on the training data

(b) **Test data.** The dataset used for the evaluation of the taxon recogniser is another BHL volume about *Coleoptera* (Beetles)[12]. Taxonomic names are annotated in two datasets of different quality text, one is *clear text* (high-quality text) and the other is the original *OCR text* with scanning errors (poor-quality text). The reason for building this comparative corpus is to estimate the impact of OCR errors on taxon name recognition. The statistics about this corpus are given in Table 2. More taxonomic names are found in the OCR text than the clear text because the OCR text includes page headings that may contain the scientific name of an organism.

	Clear Text	**OCR Text**
#Pages	373	373
#Taxonomic Names	5,198	5,414
#Taxonomic Names (with OCR error)	--	2,335 (43.1%)

Table 2. The statistics on the test data

3.2 Taxonomic Name Identification

To train the CRF-based recogniser, we used a variety of linguistic and semantic features to characterise the semantics of taxonomic names. The features used for taxon recognition were grouped into the following five categories:

- **Word-token Feature.** This type of feature includes word lemma, Part-of-Speech (POS) tag, and chunk tag of the word, which are obtained from the Genia Tagger[13].
- **Context Features.** The features for the lemma and POS tag of the three neighbouring words before and after the current word token are also considered.
- **Orthographic Features.** Taxonomic names tend to be case sensitive, e.g. *Agelaus phaenicio*. Moreover, much taxonomic literature employs abbreviations as standard like *A. phaenicio*. Some special tokens, e.g. Greek symbols (α, β, γ) and Roman numbers (*I.*, *II.*, *iv.*) also frequently occur in the text.
- **Morphologic Features.** Some taxonomic names contain typographic ligatures, e.g., *æ* (*ae*), *œ* (*oe*), *Æ* (*AE*). We observed that some mentions contain the same suffix strings such as *-us*, *-um*, *-eus*.
- **Domain-specific Features.** Taxonomic rank markers and their abbreviations, e.g., *species*, *genus*, *sp.*, *subg.*, *fam.*, etc., frequently occur in the text preceding taxonomic names. This is a binary property. *Y* if the word is a rank marker or *O* otherwise.

The training data file for the CRFs consists of a set of word token instances, each of which contains a feature vector that is made up of five groups of features described above together with an entity class label – BIO tags.

	Precision	Recall	F-measure
Clear text	0.9285	0.8642	0.8952
OCR text	0.4450	0.3716	0.4050

Table 3. The overall performance of taxonomic name identification on a comparative dataset

Performance Evaluation. The trained CRFs were evaluated on the test corpus. We compared the results of the clear text with those of the OCR text in order to test the OCR-error toleration capability of the trained CRFs. As shown in Table 3, the trained CRFs performs well and achieves an F-measure as high as 0.8952 on the clear text

[8] http://www.biodiversitylibrary.org/ia/mobotbca_12_01_01
[9] http://www.biodiversitylibrary.org/ia/mobotbca_03_01_00
[10] http://www.biodiversitylibrary.org/ia/mobotbca_05_00_00
[11] http://www.inotaxa.org/jsp/index.jsp
[12] http://www.biodiversitylibrary.org/ia/mobotbca_12_04_03
[13] http://www-tsujii.is.s.u-tokyo.ac.jp/GENIA/tagger/

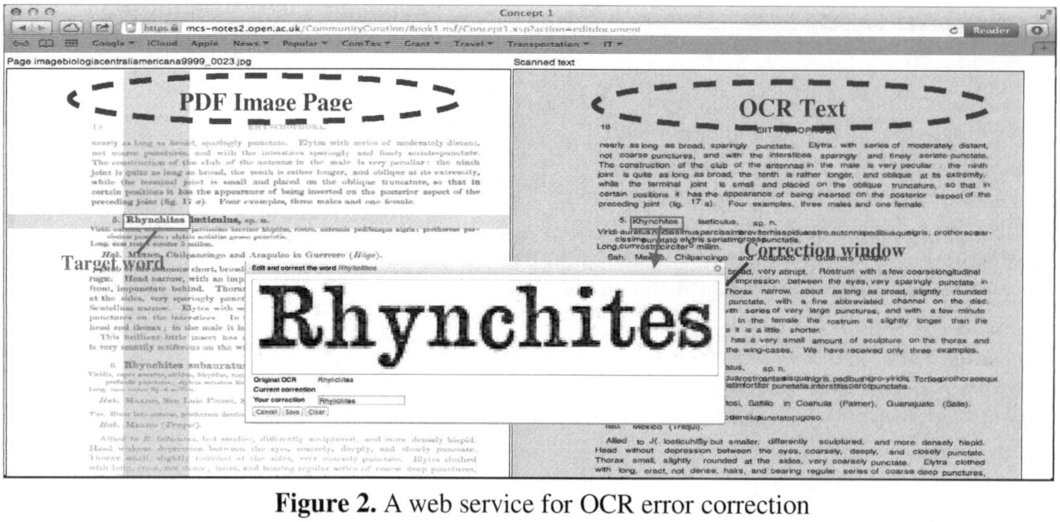

Figure 2. A web service for OCR error correction

(good-quality text). On the "dirty" OCR text the performance is worse and the F-measure drops to 0.405. This shows that OCR errors are a potential threat that greatly affects the effectiveness of taxonomic name identification. Therefore an OCR error correction tool is necessary for searching and processing the OCR-scanned text.

OCR Error Correction. To reduce the impact of OCR errors on the identification of taxonomic names, we developed a mechanism for error checking and correction. Figure 2 shows a screen shot of the web service[14] used to highlight a potential taxon to a user. The left-hand panel is the image of the original page, and the right-hand panel is the corresponding text, which is extracted from the DjVu XML file created by the OCR software. When a word is selected using the navigation content in the right-hand panel, a small error-correction window pops up, and the user is allowed to make possible modifications, based on the enlarged image of the target word appearing in the pop-up window.

3.3 Taxonomic Name Mapping

Taxonomic name mapping or normalization is to map the detected mentions in the text into standardised taxonomic identifiers (Gerner et al. (2010). It aims to generate correct lists of unique identifiers (typically from referent taxonomic databases) for each taxonomic name. There are two potential factors that affect mapping accuracy. First, taxonomic names are not completely stable, and may change due to taxonomic revision. There may be multiple names (synonyms) for the same organism, and the same name may refer to different taxa (homonyms). Moreover, there is lexical and terminological variation among taxonomic names. Second, currently there is not a complete taxonomic database that covers all the organisms in the world so multiple taxonomic databases are needed to complement each other.

To resolve the problem of orthographic and term variations between taxonomic names, we exploited a generic and effective cascaded matching method that consists of two stages:

- **Stage I - Exact Matching:** string matching between original identified mentions and database entries. If a name mention is a known synonym in the curated list of a taxonomic database, the unique identifier of a taxon entry associated with the synonym will be assigned to the mention. It is possible that the mention might be mapped to synonyms of different organisms. In these ambiguous cases, additional information such as the surrounding context of the mention and the attributes of its neighboring mentions are needed to help determine the selection of the most appropriate organism.
- **Stage II - Rule-based approximate matching:** First, a set of transformation rules that capture morphologic features of name variations are generated to produce more potential extended mentions. Second, for each unmatched mention filtered at the first stage, the possible extended candidate names created by the transformation rules (described later) are sent to the taxonomic databases again to find the possible matched synonyms of a known taxon entry.

14 http://mcs-notes2.open.ac.uk/CommunityCuration/Book1.nsf/Concept1.xsp

Construction of transformation rules. According to the observations on our manually-annotated taxonomic dataset, we roughly group name variations into the four categories below:

(a) **Ligature replacement:** typographic ligatures (e.g., æ, œ, Æ, Œ, etc.) that appear in taxonomic names of the old literature are generally replaced with the corresponding two or more consecutive letters. For example, *Agelæus phœniceus* -> *Agelaeus phoeniceus*, *Dendrœca* -> *Dendroica*

(b) **Latin declension:** the scientific name of an organism is always written in either Latin or Greek. A Latin noun can be described in different declension instances (e.g., First-declension, Second-declension) by changing its suffix substring. For instance, *puellae*, *puellarum*, *puellis*, *puellas*, can be normalized as the same root word *Puella*.

(c) **Parenthesized trinomial names:** some taxonomic names consist of three parts. These are usually represented as a species names with a subgenus name contained within parentheses, e.g., *Corvus (Pica) beecheii*, *Tanagra (Aglaia) diaconus*. However, the parenthesized subgenus name is not used very much, and some taxonomic databases do not contain the information at this low rank level. Therefore, the subgenus name can be ignored when mapping, e.g., *Corvus (Pica) beecheii* -> *Corvus beecheii*

(d) **Taxon variety names:** taxon variety names are another special case, which can appear in various name forms like *Peucæa æstivalis arizonæ*; *Peucæa æstivalis var. arizonæ*; *Peucæa æstivalis, var arizonæ*; *Peucæa æstivalis, β. Arizonæ*; even *Peucæa arizonæ* due to taxonomic inflation in which known subspecies are raised to species as a result in a change in species concept (Isaac et al. 2004).

A set of linguistic rules are expressed as regular expressions to record the syntactic and semantic clues found in the name variations discussed above. These rules are used to transform the original mentions to possible extended candidates for string matching in taxonomic databases.

External taxonomic databases. To link more identified mentions to existing external taxonomic databases, we chose three widely-used large-scale taxonomic databases: uBio Name Bank, Encyclopaedia of Life (EoL), and Catalogue of Life (CoL), which separately curate 4.8 million, 1.3 million, and 1.6 million taxonomic names respectively. In each database, each species has exactly one entry with a unique identifier, a name classified as *scientific name* (i.e. the "correct" canonical name), as well as other possible variants (e.g., synonyms, common misspellings, or retired names if the organism has been reclassified). Moreover, these three databases provide relevant web services to users for online search of taxonomic names. For each candidate name, we send a name query to different databases, and automatically extract the relevant unique identifier from the returned result.

Mapping Results. We collected a total of 8,687 distinct candidate names from four annotated BHL volumes and mapped them to the chosen taxonomic databases. Table 4 shows the statistical information of name matches in the individual databases. It is interesting to note that the matched names in EoL usually can be found in uBio, whereas CoL can find some names that do not appear in either uBio or EoL. Nearly a half of the names (4, 273 names) could not be found in any of the taxonomic databases. This suggests that machine-learning based TNR can find quite a lot of new names that a simple dictionary approach cannot identify. Moreover, biodiversity literature is a potentially useful resource to enrich the existing taxonomic databases.

	uBio	EoL	CoL
Mapped Names (total names: 8,687)	3,565 (41.1%)	2,893 (33.3%)	3,354 (38.6%)

Table 4. Name mapping in taxonomic databases

4 Community Metadata Collection

Biodiversity communities have come to the consensus that converting unstructured biodiversity literature into semantically-enabled, machine-readable structured data is essential to use the currently highly fragmented data sources. The main semantic metadata system is the Darwin Core biodiversity data standard[15], maintained by the Biodiversity Information Standards group (TDWG)[16], and based on Dublin Core. The main objects in Darwin Core represent an organism's scientific name, information pertaining to its classification, and the geographical and geological contexts of the organism.

For this research, key information can be stored in the **dwc:Taxon** class, which has terms defined for the taxonomic name itself (**dwc:scientificName**), as well as a unique identifier, the Life Sciences ID (LSID) to locate the

[15] http://rs.tdwg.org/dwc/index.htm

[16] http://www.tdwg.org/

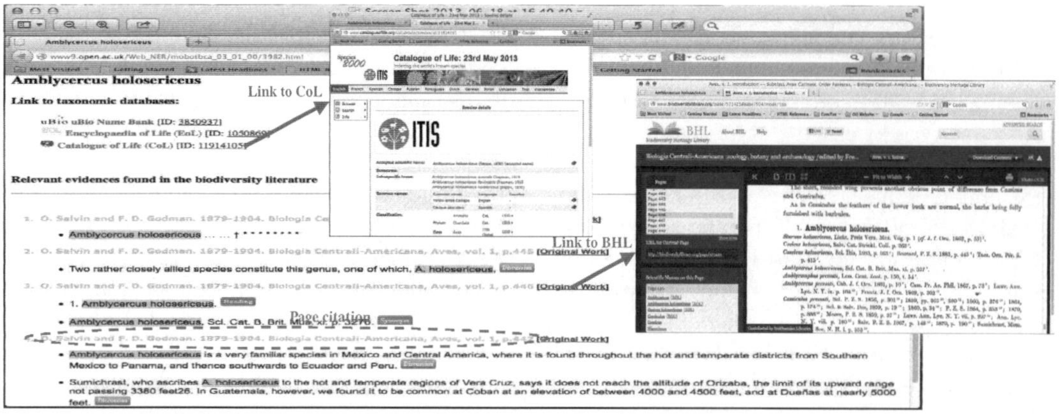

Figure 3. A sample web page to show how extracted semantic features link to the BHL and external taxonomic databases

taxon across remote databases (**dwc:taxonID**) and various terms giving taxonomic information and provenance. For example, the metadata identifying the LSID and publication data for the species *Anthus correndera* might be represented using the standard Darwin Core terms:

```
<dwc:Taxon>
  <dwc:taxonID>urn:lsid:catalogueoflife.org:
    taxon:f000e838-29c1-102b-9a4a-
     00304854f820:col20120721</dwc:taxonID>
  <dwc:scientificName>Anthus
           correndera</dwc:scientificName>
  <dwc:class>Aves</dwc:class>
  <dwc:genus>Anthus</dwc:genus>
  <dwc:specificEpithet>correndera
                  </dwc:specificEpithet>
  <dwc:namePublishedIn> London Med.
      Repos., 15: 308.</dwc:namePublishedIn>
</dwc:Taxon>
```

The basic Darwin Core terms can be extended to represent the information obtained via the original document and the curation tools. Labels should be used to represent information about the verified form of the name and the identity of the verifier, with the verifier's Scratchpad login name being the obvious choice. Adding the name of the verified form and the verifier with appropriate labels to the metadata (**dwc:nameVerifiedBy** and **dwc:dateVerified**) would then give:

```
<dwc:Taxon>
  <dwc:taxonID>urn:lsid:catalogueoflife.org:
    taxon:f000e838-29c1-102b-9a4a-
     00304854f820:col20120721</dwc:taxonID>
  <dwc:scientificName>Anthus
           correndera</dwc:scientificName>
  <dwc:nameVerifiedBy>Scratchpad user:
       Michael Smith</dwc:nameVerifiedBy>
  <dwc:dateVerified>2013-06-15
                  </dwc:dateVerified>
  <dwc:genus>Anthus</dwc:genus>
  <dwc:specificEpithet>correndera
                  </dwc:specificEpithet>
  <dwc:namePublishedIn>London Med.
      Repos., 15: 308.</dwc:namePublishedIn>
</dwc:Taxon>
```

Further contextual information can be stored, providing species description information including morphological features, biogeographic distribution, and ecology. Figure 3 shows a web page[17] corresponding to a species in which the contexts surrounding the occurrence of the target mention are extracted from the text. Each piece of evidence is given a bibliographic citation that is linked to the respective copy of the referring page (here, the BHL). Unique database identifiers and hyperlinks to external taxonomic databases are provided on the web page if possible. Connections to external databases increase the understanding and analysis of the behaviour of the target species. These bibliographic linkages allow the system to identify and track back the raw data across the range of remote databases.

The metadata can potentially encode many semantic aspects of the data. Identified taxonomic names and hyperlinks to repositories will improve species-specific document retrieval. Encoding different names for organisms will improve synonym detection so reconciliation techniques are needed to connect multiple names. Also, linkages to the unique identifiers of organisms facilitate the reconciliation process. Future work will consider citation information, which improves the traceability of naming authorities.

[17] http://www9.open.ac.uk/Web_NER/mobotbca_03_01_00/3982.html

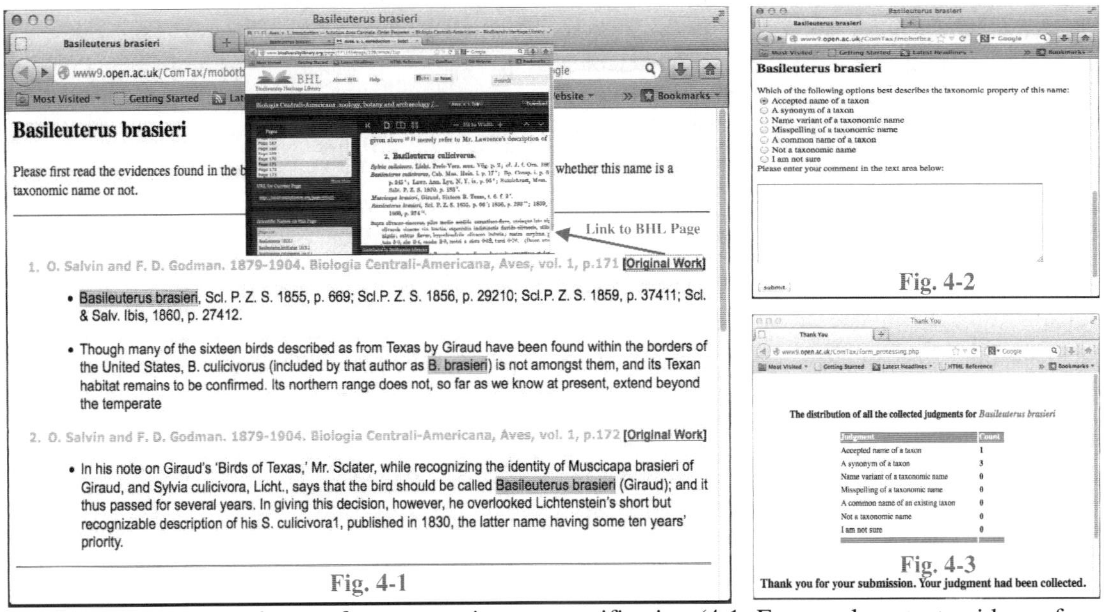

Figure 4. A sample web page for taxonomic name verification (4-1: Extracted context evidence from the text; 4-2: A multi-option form for judgment collection; 4-3: The distribution of human judgments)

4.1 Taxonomic Name Validation

Taxonomic name validation task is to present unknown names for human validation. Validating taxonomic names is a specialist process, requiring extensive human involvement and expertise. Non-professional taxonomists and citizen scientists are an essential part of this effort. We aim to demonstrate how small, lightweight plugins integrated to existing web-based collaboration tools can facilitate the semantic annotation of open biodiversity resources via crowdsourcing techniques.

Scratchpads (Smith et al. 2009) are a content management system that is optimised for handling biological taxonomy data. Scratchpads are widely used amongst professional and amateur taxonomists, and so are a useful portal for validation.

Our curation web service is a Scratchpads plug-in. Text for validation is selected via a simple recommender system[18] (Figure 4). Users are presented with one or more potential taxonomic names found by the CRFs, as text "snippets" containing the proposed name with the surrounding context of the original scan (Figure 4-1). To collect specialists' judgments, a multiple-option form (Figure 4-2) is used to request a judgment of whether the text snippet represents a potentially new taxon, a synonym or a name variant of an existing organism.

The validation information is collected in a back-end MySQL database in a metadata format that contains the curator's name, verification time stamp, the target name, the associated publication, along with appropriate page citations and associated URI page linkages to make the support evidence traceable. By ensuring that this data is available to the community via the semantic web service layer, the judgment is exposed to the community for further validation or modification (distribution illustrated in Figure 4-3).

Our aim in the medium term is to link the validation task to search results within the Scratchpad portal[19]. This will allow us to investigate whether the output of document searching can be used as a reward for carrying out the validation exercise, and so whether the task can be presented in a (relatively) unobtrusive manner to users.

5 Conclusions and Future Work

Increasing numbers of older documents are scanned and made available online, through digital heritage projects like BHL. It will become more important to annotate those documents with semantic data in order to curate and manage the information contained in the documents.

We have described how information extraction techniques can be used as part of a curation system to improve the mechanisms for collecting

18 http://www9.open.ac.uk/ComTax/mobotbca_03_01_00/4136.html

19 http://taxoncuration.myspecies.info/node/77

this metadata. Although we have focused on identifying taxonomic names, the same techniques could be used to recognise any data of interest, such as geographical data in historic land documents, or proper names in census data. The critical part of the system, of course, is to be able to find suitable user groups to provide the appropriate semantic markup, as the data can rapidly become very large.

The semantic web can provide a portal to this data, if the metadata can be reliably collected. We believe that IE-supported curation techniques can be used to bring this collection about.

Future work includes: (1) The datasets were annotated by one computer scientist. It would be interesting to compare the annotated data with the verification results from biodiversity experts. (2) We need more annotated OCR text for the development of an automated OCR-error correction tool and a TNR tool built for OCR text. (3) Our project is in its early stages and requires more time for the collection of validation judgments; to conduct the evaluation of the validation tool and to analyse the validation results.

Acknowledgments

The work was funded by JISC through the Digital Infrastructure programme, Managing Research Data call. We thank Mr Jef Lay for developing the OCR error correction tool shown in Figure 2.

References

L. M. Akella, C. N. Norton, and H. Miller. 2012. NetiNeti: discovery of scientific names from text using machine learning methods. *BMC Bioinformatics,* 13 (211):1471-2105.

M. Gerner, G. Nenadic, and C. M. Bergman. 2010. LINNAEUS: A Species Name Identification System for Biomedical Literature. *BMC Bioinformatics* 11:85.

H. C. Godfray. 2002. Challenges for taxonomy. *Nature,* 417 (6884):17-19.

N. J. Isaac, J. Mallet, and G. M. Mace. 2004. Taxonomic inflation: its influence on macroecology and conservation. *Trends in Ecology and Evolution.* 19: 464–469.

D. Koning, N. Sarkar, and T. Moritz. 2005. Taxongrab: extracting taxonomic names from text. *Biodiversity Informatics,* 2:79–82.

J. Lafferty, A. McCallum, and F. Pereira. 2001. Conditional random fields: Probabilistic models for segmenting and labeling sequence data. In *Proceedings of the International Conference on Machine Learning (ICML-2001),* pages 282-289.

P. R. Leary, D. P. Remsen, C. N. Norton, D. J. Patterson, and I. N. Sarkar. 2007. uBioRSS: tracking taxonomic literature using RSS. *Bioinformatics,* 23(11):1434–1436.

R. D. M. Page. 2006. Taxonomic Names, Metadata, and The Semantic Web. *Biodiversity Informatics,* 3, pp. 1-15.

L. Penev, D. Agosti, T. Georgiev, et al. 2010. Semantic tagging of and semantic enhancements to systematics papers: ZooKeys working examples. *ZooKeys,* 50:1–16.

D. Remsen. 2011. Biodiversity Informatics - GBIFs role in linking information through scientific names. In *The Symposium of Anchoring Biodiversity Information: From Sherborne to the 21st Century and Beyond.*

I. N. Sarkar. 2007. Biodiversity informatics: organizing and linking information across the spectrum of life. *Briefings in Bioinformatics,* 8(5):347-357.

G. Sautter, K. Böhm, and D. Agosti. 2006. A combining approach to find all taxon names (FAT) in legacy biosisystematics literature. *Biodiversity informatics,* 3:41-53.

Secretariat of the Convention on Biological Diversity (SCBD). 2008. *Guide to the global taxonomy initiative.* CBD, Technical Report.

V. Smith, S. Rycroft, K. Harman, B. Scott, and D. Roberts. 2009. Scratchpads: A Data-Publishing Framework to Build, Share and Manage Information on the Diversity of Life. *BMC Bioinformatics* 10(14):S6.

P. Stenetorp, S. Pyysalo, G. Topić, T. Ohta, S. Ananiadou, and J. Tsujii. 2012. brat: a Web-based Tool for NLP-Assisted Text Annotation. In *Proceedings of the Demonstrations Session at EACL 2012*, pages 102-107.

Q. Wei, P. B. Heidorn, and C. Freeland. 2010. Name Matters: Taxonomic Name Recognition (TNR) in Biodiversity Heritage Library (BHL). In *Proceedins of* 2010 *iConference,* pages 284-288.

R. J. White. 2007. Linking Biodiversity Databases. *Systematics Association Special Volume,* 73:111–128.

A. Willis, D. Morse, A. Dil, D. King, D. Roberts, and C. Lyal. 2009. Improving search in scanned documents: Looking for OCR mismatches. In *Proceedings of the workshop on Advanced Technologies for Digital Libraries*, 2009.

H. Yang, G. Nenadic, and J. Keane. 2008. Identification of Transcription Factor Contexts in Literature Using Machine Learning Approaches. *BMC Bioinformatics* 9:S11.

Exploring the inference role in automatic information extraction from texts

Denis A. de Araujo, Sandro J. Rigo
PIPCA, UNISINOS
denis.andrei.araujo@gmail.com,
rigo@unisinos.br

Carolina Muller, Rove Chishman
PPGLA, UNISINOS
São Leopoldo - Brazil
muller.carolina@ymail.com,
rove@unisinos.br

Abstract

In this paper we present a novel methodology for automatic information extraction from natural language texts, based on the integration of linguistic rules, multiple ontologies and inference resources, integrated with an abstraction layer for linguistic annotation and data representation. The SAURON system was developed to implement and integrate the methodology phases. The knowledge domain of legal realm has been used for the case study scenario through a corpus collected from the State Superior Court website in Brazil. The main contribution presented is related to the exploration of the flexibility of linguistic rules and domain knowledge representation, through their manipulation and integration by a reasoning system. Therefore, it is possible to the system to continuously interact with linguistic and domain experts in order to improve the set of linguistic rules or the ontology components. The results from the case study indicate that the proposed approach is effective for the legal domain.

1 Introduction

The aim of Information Extraction (IE) field is to develop tools and methodologies to identify, annotate and extract specific information from natural language text documents. Although the efforts in this field are not recent (Rillof, 2009), its growing importance and necessity certainly are related to the large volume of natural language text documents and relevant textual information currently stored in databases. Due to this context, the manual analysis of these resources becomes unfeasible. Therefore, text documents automatic processing stands as a necessity and the achievement of better results in IE systems allow improvements in the effectiveness of other related systems, such as, for instance, the Information Retrieval systems.

The initial systems of IE generally were related to specific domains as a way to achieve better results in their operation. Some of the main aspects considered by these IE systems are the frequency and position of domain-related terms (Wimalasurya, 2009). Related to these approach, some well-known works in the area (Bruninghaus, 2001; Jijkoun, 2004) do not consider certain important relation descriptions concerning linguistic and domain knowledge aspects. Recently, aiming to improve the flexibility and precision in IE, the use of domain knowledge, expressed by ontologies, is observed in several approaches (Saravanan, 2009; Daya 2010). Some other initiatives incorporate linguistic aspects in their design (Wyner, 2011; Moens, 1999; Amardeihl, 2005) in order to better treat natural language complex structures.

This paper presents a novel methodology for Information Extraction from natural language texts that combine domain knowledge with linguistic knowledge. The linguistics information is represented in form of ontologies and allows the application of automated reasoning algorithms. Therefore some improvements over related work are achieved. The first one is the wide use of semantic information described in domain ontologies, allowing reuse and the integration of multiple ontologies. The second is the incorporation of linguistic information, which is obtained from studies of the domain documents, composing flexible and precise rules for information extraction. The last one is the extensive use of an inference system, in order to integrate and process textual, domain and linguistic information. Moreover, an abstraction layer for linguistic annotation and data representation (Chiarcos, 2012a) is adopted as a key component of the methodology. The main benefit from this choice is the greater flexibility in the integration and processing of different parser originated annotations, as well as some facilities in the use of corpora originated from different sources.

The work has been developed in the context of a research group within the scope of the project "Semantic technologies and legal information retrieval systems"[1]. The group involved in this project aims to develop a conceptual-semantic model of the Brazilian legal domain, in order to integrate it into Information Retrieval systems targeted at legal documentation. The group has an interdisciplinary composition, comprising lawyers, linguists and computer science researchers.

2 Related Work

In this section we present two aspects of related works. The first one is more general and not related to IE techniques, but illustrates the increasing availability of data collections and data repositories, some of them fully integrated with several databases. The second aspect is related to the technical differences of the proposed approach from previous works.

There is a trend in providing facilitated access to documents in several specific domains and in the adoption of some standards to describe document collections. Therefore, these initiatives foster the generation of document patterns and repositories for annotation and automatic processing.

Since the case study adopted in this work is dedicated to the legal realm, some relevant examples of this situation are mentioned here. Currently, there are several initiatives underway to achieve a standard representation of legal documents, aimed at facilitating their automatic processing. In Brazil, LEXML project[2] is concerned with information representation and information retrieval, as well as some other projects in Italy also care about those issues (Brighi, 2009; Biagioli, 2005; Palmirani 2011). Some other examples of projects in this area can be cited, as the Institute of Legal Information Theory and Techniques[3], the results of Estrella Project[4] and Metalex standard proposal[5]. In general, standards and schemes are used in these initiatives, implemented in flexible formats, such as XML[6], fostering the generation of patterns for annotation and access. The existence of this trend in providing affordable computational formats shows the correct positioning of efforts to create automatic tools for legal text treatment.

Regarding the technical aspects, it is important to identify the main differences presented by the proposed methodology from previous works, which resides mainly in the representation of linguistic information in form of ontologies and in the extensive use of inference mechanisms and linguistic rules to identify relevant events. This novel approach was not found in the reviewed material and it brings to the implemented system the possibilities of achieving better precision and flexibility, as described in the results analysis.

Some initial efforts in Information Extraction for legal realm were conceived with the same syntactic pattern approach observed in other fields (Jijkoun, 2004; Oard, 2010). These works presents no capability to cope with some important linguistic relations and also lack flexibility to maintain the sets of syntactic patterns used.

To overcome such aspects, some works apply knowledge representation as a resource to improve the domain information possibilities, since the IE is dependent of specific vocabulary and related to proper concepts. The use of ontologies is adopted in several works (Saravanan, 2009; Soysal, 2010) and allow improvements in domain concepts representation. In such works, in general, the ontologies are mainly used as concepts repositories, dedicated to help in search operations, therefore with little exploration of inference and reasoning possibilities.

The linguistics information is also applied in several works (Moens, 1999; Mazzei, 2009; Cederberg, 2003) and these approaches contribute to the understanding of the great importance of using linguistic structures in IE, since they allow a more precise analysis of the texts. Extending these initiatives, some proposals suggest the use of ontologies combined with linguistic analysis (Amardeilh, 2005; Palmirani, 2011; Lenci, 2007). The main argument in these cases is the possible improvements integrating the linguistic and domain knowledge, providing a better basis to the text analysis. In these approaches, however, there is not an integrated representation of the domain knowledge and the linguistic analysis, as provided by the proposed methodology in this work.

3 Proposed methodology

The proposed methodology has two phases, called linguistic phase and computational phase. In the first one the focus of attention is the cor-

[1] Legal Research Support Program No. 020/2010/CAPES/CNJ
[2] http://projeto.lexml.gov.br
[3] http://www.ittig.cnr.it/
[4] http://www.estrellaproject.org/
[5] http://www.metalex.eu/
[6] http://www.w3.org/XML/

pus study, which is necessary to build the necessary domain ontology and linguistic rules. The second phase objective is to integrate linguistic rules with domain ontologies through the use of an inference system and the abstraction layer for linguistic annotation and data representation. This phase is therefore based on the use of Natural Language Processing techniques (LIDDY, 2003), ontology and inference resources. The outcome of this phase is a knowledge base composed by the relevant information identified.

To illustrate the overall methodology integration aspects, the Figure 1 shows the main elements of each phase. As indicated in the Figure 1, in the linguistic phase the desired corpus is studied and then are generated two ontologies: the ontology with the linguistic rules and the domain ontology. The linguistic rules, depending on their complexity, are formalized in OWL (McGuinness, 2004), through logical axioms in Description Logic (Baader, 2003) or SWRL[7]. The domain ontology is formalized in OWL language.

The computational phase aims to provide the text documents processing and the integration of the domain ontology with the ontology containing the linguistic rules. We propose in our methodology that the natural language text documents submitted to the IE process should be first treated by a deep linguistic parser and then represented in OWL with the POWLA data model (Chiarcos, 2012). This data model represents corpora structures through linguistic concepts in OWL, therefore allowing the use of the linguistic rules and the domain ontology concepts in an integrated and flexible manner. When necessary, some optimizations can be performed in order to ensure that the represented text do not generate excessive and not useful information.

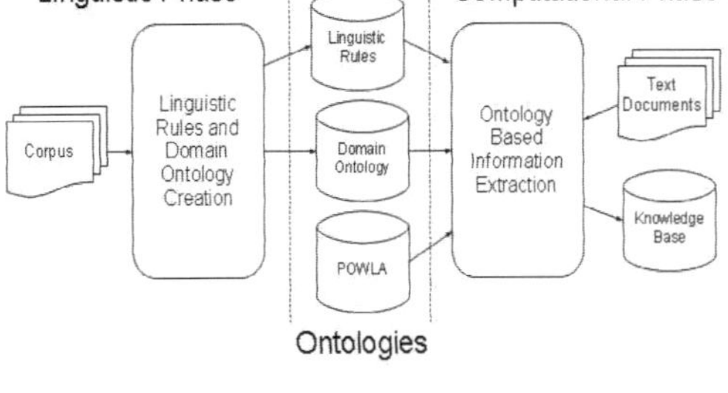

Figure 1. General view of the proposed methodology phases

As an outcome of these methodological choices, we can indicated the following positive aspects: (a) the IE process can be done with data originated from different linguistic parsers; (b) the linguistic rules can be formulated considering more than one annotation layer; (c) the reasoning system integrates the description of the domain, the linguistic rules and the documents linguistic annotation; (d) the knowledge representation of linguistic rules, domain and linguistic annotation can be manipulated in a flexible way. Some details in the proposed methodology are described below.

3.1 Domain Ontology construction

In general, IE is context dependent, since there are specific vocabulary and textual constructions more frequently observed in each knowledge field. Due to this situation, our methodology applies domain ontology to describe the important concepts of the targeted area. This domain ontology is created through a semantic analysis of terms and their relations, during the study of natural language texts describing the desired domain area.

We consider that using the domain ontology together with linguistic rules can improve precision and recall in the computational phase. One of the main aspects supporting this consideration is the integration of concepts and relations described in the domain ontology with elements of the linguistic rules ontology, thus allowing greater accuracy.

Also it is important to note that the reuse aspect of ontologies can be a very important element to foster the methodology application in different knowledge domains. In the case study related in this work, aiming at the legal realm, the domain ontology was created using the categories recommended by (Minghelli, 2011), that are: Legal Events, Legal Institutions, Legal Documents and Legal Participants.

With these categories, is possible to capture and describe specific contexts that assist in the interpretation of textual information found in the text documents. It also enables the identification of various important relations, such as dependency and composition. The integration established between the domain ontology and the linguistic rules foster the specification of references between elements described in the domain ontology and linguistic elements.

3.2 Description of Linguistic Rules

Linguistic experts define the linguistic rules applied in our methodology, in order to better represent the knowledge involved in textual analy-

[7] http://www.w3.org/Submission/SWRL/

sis. The experts in the knowledge field are also involved in this phase.

Therefore, the linguistic rules represent the reflections of the linguistic experts about the textual constructions, based on linguistic corpus analysis and interactions with other experts in the knowledge area.

In order to achieve flexibility and to maintain the greater amount of semantic information, in our methodology, the linguistic rules will be expressed in sets of constructions in Description Logic and SWRL rules. These rules also combine the concepts of the domain ontology, and therefore are able to correctly and precisely identify terms and excerpts of the text documents analyzed.

These documents are represented using the POWLA/OWL data model. One of the advantages of this approach is the flexibility for describing linguistic rules. Since the basic elements of the text are available, together with more complex components, such as sentences or phrasal structures, the linguistic rules can be expressed using all these aspects. This expands the possibilities of the linguists in the description of the rules. This context is possible through the use of multiple ontologies, which are specialized in different components, such as the annotation layer, the domain concepts, and the linguistic rules specification.

Despite the higher computational cost that this approach can present when compared with some other options, the results, as described in the result analysis section, presents a good precision and are not dependent of a large volume of documents to generate basic and reference models.

3.3 Computational Phase: the SAURON System

The computational phase of the methodology suggested is implemented in the SAURON system, developed in Java Language[8] and the OWL Api[9] support, integrating the Pellet reasoner[10].

This system is inspired in the unifying logic layer of the standard technology stack for semantic web[11], since one of the objectives of this system is to unify the use of several semantic technologies applied. The system provides the necessary support to the tasks involving Natural Language Processing, such as the text preprocessing, the syntactic parser access and some format conversions tasks.

The first computational process performed on the text documents is to convert them to OWL representation. To do this, we first apply the widely adopted Palavras parser (Bick, 2000), which is a morph-syntactic parser for Portuguese. The result produced by the parser after the text document analysis is a file in TIGER-XML format (König, 2003). This file contains a hierarchical structure of the sentences from the original document and the linguistic annotations (Bick, 2005) about terms that compose them. TIGER-XML file has many linguistic annotations that represent a rich source of data to carry out the identification of information in automated systems.

The large amount of linguistic information generated by linguistic parser will be used to make ontological inferences. To accomplish this we used the POWLA data model to convert the TIGER-XML format to OWL. For this task we adapted a script developed originally to convert documents from TIGER-XML to POWLA (Chiarcos 2012a). After this initial processing of the texts, the SAURON System integrates the textual information, the ontologies containing the linguistic rules and the domain knowledge produced at linguistic phase. This is done through a process of ontologies integration and the use of the inference engine, responsible for identifying the concepts in the text documents processed.

4 Experiment description

To obtain and evaluate results with the use of the developed methodology, we conducted an experiment in the legal realm. To better demonstrate the methodology aspects, the next sections describe the domain ontology created, then some of the linguistic rules construction and, finally, the obtained results. The experiment was conducted with a corpus of 200 documents, composed of 39.895 sentences, that was obtained from RS State Superior Court (in Portuguese, *Tribunal Superior do Rio Grande do Sul - TJRS*). The results of the automatic extraction of events were manually reviewed by experts for the identification of its correction and to latter recall and precision metrics application.

4.1 Domain ontology creation

To implement the tasks of the linguistic phase in this case study, we adopted the following methodology: selection of corpus, relevant term ex-

[8] http://docs.oracle.com/javase/

[9] http://owlapi.sourceforge.net/

[10] http://clarkparsia.com/pellet/

[11] http://www.w3.org/2001/12/semweb-fin/w3csw

traction, choice of ontology terms, definition of hierarchy and relations as well as formalization of the ontology in the Protégé[12] editor. Experts in linguistics, law and knowledge representation did this task.

The next step was to find verb`s definition for a better semantic description. The participation of research group´s law experts was essential in the determination and description of the events to better represent the domain knowledge. We also made use of a Legal Vocabulary dictionary (Silva, 2009) to clarify the meaning of terms related to legal events. Considering the verbs extracted from the corpus and their meaning, a list of legal events evoked by each one was defined. Having clearly defined verbs and events, we moved on to the semantic analysis based on Lexical Semantics (Cruse, 2000) to establish a taxonomic relation between events and verbs.

The relations of hyponymy and synonymy stood out, guiding the organization in terms of ontology. In addition, we performed a parsing of sentences to verify participants involved in the event. The last part of this process was to include detected events, participants and verbs in Protégé[11] ontology editor. Closing the study phase of the linguistic corpus, the domain ontology was structured including legal events found in the analyzed corpus. That ontology resulted in 95 axioms, being 51 logical axioms, 41 classes (3 main and 38 subclasses), with 7 axioms of class equivalence.

4.2 Linguistic rules description

In this study case our objective was to automatically identify the legal events *Denúncia* (formal charges), *Absolvição* (acquittal), *Condenação* (conviction) and *Interrogatório* (questioning). These are the main events described in the domain ontology created for the experiment.

The linguistic analysis of phrases intends to identify linguistic patterns, which will lead to the creation of the linguistic rules used to identify these legal events. This process will be illustrated in details through the analysis of the phrase in Figure 2, which was extracted from one of the case study documents. This phrase describes one example of the *Denúncia* event.

The excerpt from Figure 2 presents a simple linguistic pattern typical of phrases containing the event Formal Charges in its verbal form. So, we identified that the presence of the verb *Denunciar* (present formal charges, in English) is an indication of the presence of the event.

However, we must seek other linguistic marks, because the verb alone is not sufficient to conclude the presence or absence of the event. In the sentence being analyzed in Figure 2, we see that the agent of the verb is the Prosecutor, indicating that the verb expresses the meaning we want to identify.

> *"O Ministério Público denunciou NNNN como incurso nas sanções do artigo 121, § 2o, inciso IV, do Código Penal."*
>
> *(in English:* "Prosecutors charged NNNN according to the article 121, paragraph 2, item (IV), of the Penal Code.")

Figure 2. Excerpt referring to *DENÚNCIA* (formal charges).

The above findings lead us to define that phrases containing the verb *DENUNCIAR* whose agent is the Prosecutor refer the event *DENÚNCIA* (formal charges). These conclusions will be represented in the form of linguistic rules. The information required for the elaboration of the linguistic rules are generated by the Portuguese language parser Palavras [Bick 2000], which provides various information ranging from the sentence analyzed through labeling and classifying words and phrases.

The Figure 3 shows part of the the linguistic information generated by the Palavras parser, but now represented in OWL language through the POWLA data model. In the Figure 3 we can see the integration of the syntactic and structural information. This structural information aims to represent, for example, the relations of the term described as "s1_7" with other phrase components, such as the components described as nextNode, previousNode, hasRoot, isTargetOf and hasParent. These components are part of the annotation layer of the POWLA data model.

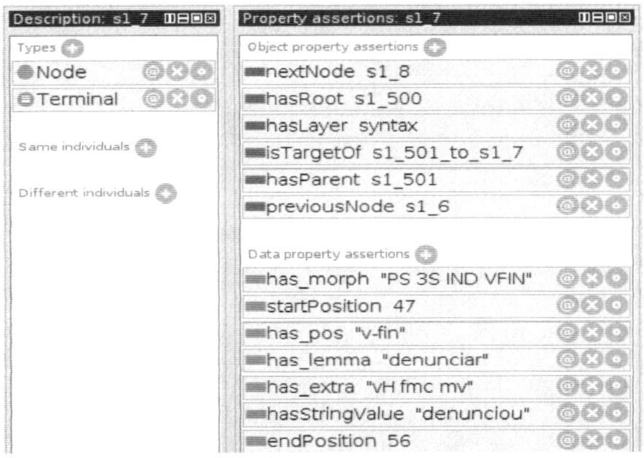

Figure 3. Linguistic information in OWL using POWLA data model.

---

12 http://protege.stanford.edu/

The use of OWL language to represent the linguistic information of the text documents makes possible to use Description Logic or SWRL to formalize the linguistic rules. A linguistic rule to identify the verb *denunciar*, for example, can be described in a simple way: all the individuals of the Terminal class containing the term which canonical form (lemma) is *denunciar* can be considered examples of this form.

The rule for the identification of examples of the *denunciar* verb can be defined in a Description Logic axiom as illustrated in Figure 4. The POWLA's data property has_lemma, which corresponds to the tag lemma of TIGER-XML, contains the canonical form of the word. This makes it possible to define that any individual Terminal class, whose has_lemma property is *denunciar*, is also an instance of the class *Denunciar*.

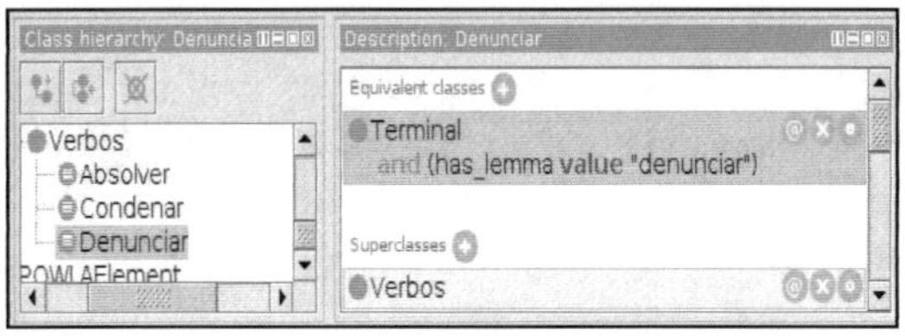

Figure 4. Linguistic Rule to identify the verb denunciar

The other essential element for assessing the presence of the event is the agent of the verb. By definition, we know that the agent of the *denunciar* verb should be *Ministério Público* (Prosecutor, in English). The linguistic rule for identification of this entity on text is also simple and can be represented by another Description Logic axiom. The Figure 5 shows this linguistic rule using Manchester syntax (Horridge, 2006).

```
Class: Ministério_Público
Equivalent to:
        Terminal
        and (has_lemmavalue "Ministério_Público")
```

Figure 5. DL linguistic rule to identify *Ministério Público* (*Prosecutor*).

Now that we have the linguistic rules for the identification of the two main components of *Denúncia* event, we can define the linguistic relations between them to verify if the event is referenced at the analyzed phrases. As this rule is more complex and requires a more expressive set of elements, it is formalized in SWRL. Figure 6 shows an example of the SWRL rule, that use the information generated by linguistic parser. This rule uses both structural (hasParent, isSourceOf, hasTarget and hasChild) and syntactical (has_label) information.

```
1. Denunciar(?verbo),
2. hasParent(?verbo, ?fcl),
3. isSourceOf(?fcl, ?relation),
4. has_label(?relVAux, "S"^^string),
5. hasTarget(?relVAux, ?np),
6. hasChild(?np,?mp)
7. Ministério_Público(?mp)
8. -> Denúncia(?fcl)
```

Figure 6. SWRL linguistic rule to identify *Denúncia* (present formal charge).

At lines 1 and 7 in the Figure 6 are illustrated the use of the previously defined Description Logic rules (*Denunciar* and *Ministério_Público*), in an approach that foster the reuse of some basic rules in order to build more complex ones. In the line 8 of the rule is expressed the obtained conclusion: the *Denúncia* event is present in the phrase analyzed. The defined linguistic rules are inserted in an OWL file apart from the domain ontology, therefore maintaining the separation between the ontology containing concepts and the other one containing linguistic rules.

To perform this experiment were generated 12 linguistic rules, aiming to identify the main events of interest. These rules allow also the treatment of linguistic aspects, such as, for instance, the use of passive voice. The phase described in this section is a very simple one, but the methodology allow the treatment of complex linguistic structures as well. For instance, the implemented rules can deal with relations beyond verb and subject ones, exploring the linguistic information generated by the Palavras parser. Also the rules make use of the domain ontology components, both in order to generate the resulting knowledge base and to relate specific concepts.

5 Results Analysis

For the development of the case study presented here, two corpuses were elaborated, being originated from documents returned by a query performed at jurisprudence search tool available at State Superior Court TJRS website. The first one was called learning corpus, because it was used to elaborate the linguistic rules used in the experiment. This corpus consists of 10 judgments, covering the decisions published by 4 different judges. The number of sentences in the corpus is 1.861 and the number of words is 6.142.

The testing corpus had the same origin that the learning corpus, but this time 200 documents were selected and the judgments of the learning corpus were not used. The testing corpus had 39.895 sentences, 618.892 words, covering decisions taken by 19 judges.

In order to identify the events in the text documents, the domain ontology and the linguistic rules ontology are merged with the OWL file containing the linguistic information from the original text, described in POWLA format. Then the Pellet reasoner is triggered, resulting in the evaluation of the rules and in the identification of the existing events.

All the steps are performed in the context of the Sauron system. This system is fully implemented, with all the features necessary to the proposed methodology.

Comparing the results of our approach against the manually parsed set of the text documents, we have the precision and recall results shown in Table 1.

The precision metric stands for the number of correctly identified events, given the number of identified ones. The recall metric stands for the number of events identified correctly, given the total number of existent events.

The good results in the precision of events identification can be associated with the use of rules based on linguistic information. The previous documents study by experts and the broad use of parser generated linguistic information allows the creation of linguistic rules with good accuracy. The recall results present also a good outcome.

Further analysis of the text documents and the linguistic rules applied shows that these results can be improved. In our analysis, they are dependent on the available rules and, therefore, the inclusion of some additional specific rules can improve these results.

Table 1. Results from test set legal documents

Brazilian Legal Event	Equivalent English Term	Precision (%)	Recall (%)
Denúncia	Formal charges	100	92
Absolvição	Acquittal	96	90
Condenação	Conviction	98	84
Interrogatório	Questioning	100	100

The performance achieved in terms of recall indicated that the solution proposed here has a good level of generalization, which is enough to use them in the real world applications. The proportion between the learning and the testing corpora used in this experiment, and the results presented in Table 1, indicate that the suggested methodology can be successfully used on a wider scale.

The tests were conducted in a computer with 32 Gbytes of memory, equipped with Xeon processor and running Windows Server operational system. The mean size of the processed documents after the conversion to POWLA data model increase in 318% and their mean is 231 Kbytes size. The computational effort to run the reasoning system is feasible, since the mean time to process the documents is 79 seconds.

6 Conclusions and Future Work

The approach presented here indicates important perspectives, evidenced in the aspects of accuracy and recall observed in experiment. These results are associated with the integration between the linguistic and computational phases, allowing effective results and flexibility.

This work is in continuous development, with experiments planned to provide the model verification in some different domain, such as the educational domain and the medical domain.

References

Amardeilh, F., Laublet, P. and Minel, J. L. 2005. Document Annotation and Ontology Population from Linguistic Extractions, Proceedings of Knowledge Capture (KCAP), Banff.

Baader, F., Calvanese, D., McGuinness, D., Nardi, D. and Patel-Schneider, P. F. 2003. The Description Logic Handbook: Theory, Implementation and Applications, Cambridge University Press.

Bick, E. 2000. The Parsing System Palavras: Automatic Grammatical Analysis of Portuguese in a Constraint Grammar Framework, Aarhus University Press.

Bick, E. 2005. Gramática Constritiva na Análise Automática da Sintaxe Portuguesa in T. B. Sardinha, A Língua Portuguesa no Computador, Mercado das Letras, Campinas.

Brighi, R. and Palmirani, M. 2009. Legal Text Analysis of the Modification Provisions: A Pattern Oriented Approach, Proceedings of the 12th International Conference on Artificial Intelligence and Law, ICAIL '09, pages 238–239, ACM, New York, NY, USA.

Bruninghaus, S. and Ashley, K. 2001. Improving the Representation of Legal Case Texts with Information Extraction Methods, Proceedings of the 8th International Conference on Artificial Intelligence and Law (ICAIL '01), pages 42-51, ACM Press.

Biagioli, C., Francesconi, E., Passerini, A., Montemagni, S. and Soria, C. 2005. Automatic Semantics Extraction in Law Documents, Proceedings of the 10th International Conference on Artificial Intelligence and Law, ICAIL '05, pages 133–140, ACM, New York, NY, USA.

Cederberg, S. Widdows, D. 2003. Using LSA and noun coordination information to improve the precision and recall of automatic hyponymy extraction. In Proceedings of the seventh conference on Natural language learning at HLT-NAACL 2003 - Volume 4 (CONLL '03), Vol. 4. Association for Computational Linguistics, Stroudsburg, PA, USA, 111-118.

Chiarcos, C. 2012 a. Interoperability of Corpora and Annotations, in C. Chiarcos, S. Nordhoff, and S. Hellmann, editors, Linked Data in Linguistics, Representing and Connecting Language Data and Language Metadata, pages 161–179, Springer, Heidelberg.

Chiarcos, C. 2012. POWLA: Modeling Linguistic Corpora in OWL/DL, Proc. 9th Extended Semantic Web Conference (ESWC), Heraklion, Crete.

Cruse, D. A. 2000. Meaning in Language: an Introduction to Semantics and Pragmatics, Oxford University Press, New York.

Daya C. Wimalasuriya and Dejing Dou, "Ontology-based information extraction: an introduction and a survey of current approaches," Journal of Information Science, vol. 36, no. 3, pp. 306–323, 2010.

Horridge, M., Drummond, N., Goodwin, J., Rector, A., Stevens, R. and Wang, H. H. 2006. The Manchester OWL Syntax, Proc. of the OWL Experiences and Directions Workshop (OWLED) at the ISWC.

Jijkoun, V., Rijke, M. and Mur, J. 2004. Information extraction for question answering: improving recall through syntactic patterns. In Proceedings of the 20th international conference on Computational Linguistics (COLING '04).

König, E. and Lezius, W. 2003. The TIGER Language - A Description Language For Syntax Graphs, Formal definition, Technical Report.

Lenci, A., Montemagni, S., Pirrelli, V. and Venturi, G. 2007. NLP-Based Ontology Learning From Legal Texts - A Case Study, Proceedings of LOAIT , 2007.

LIDDY, R. NaturalLanguage Processing, Library and Information Science, Marcel Drecker Inc. New York, USA, 2a Ed. 2003.

Minghelli, T. D. 2011. A Relação de Meronímia em uma Ontologia Jurídica, Dissertação de Mestrado, UNISINOS, São Leopoldo.

Moens, M., Uyttendaele, C. and Dumortier, J. 1999. Information Extraction from Legal Texts: The Potential of Discourse Analysis, International Journal of Human-Computer Studies 51 (1999), 1155–1171.

Mazzei, A., Radicioni, D. P. and Brighi, R. 2009. NLP-Based Extraction of Modificatory Provisions Semantics, Proceedings of the 12th International Conference on Artificial Intelligence and Law (ICAIL), pages 50–57, Barcelona, Spain.

McGuinness, D. and van Harmelen, F. 2004. OWL Web Ontology Language Overview, W3C recommendation, http://www.w3.org/TR/owl-features (accessed 31 August 2012).

Oard, D. W., Baron, J. R., Hedin, B., Lewis, D. D. and Tomlinson, S. 2010.Evaluation of Information Retrieval for E-Discovery, Artificial Intelligence and Law.

Palmirani, M., Ceci, M., Radicioni, D. and Mazzei, A. 2011."FrameNet Model of the Suspension of Norms", In Proceedings of ICAIL 2011, pp. 189–93, New York: ACM Press.

Rillof, E., Information Extraction as a stepping stone toward story understanding. Understanding Language Understanding: computational models of reading.p.435-460, MIT Press. 1999Silva, P. 2009. Vocabulário jurídico, Forense, Rio de Janeiro.

Saravanan, M., Ravindran, B. and Raman, S. 2009. Improving Legal Information Retrieval Using an Ontological Framework, Springer Science Business Media B.V.

Soysal, E. Cicekli, I. Baykal, N. 2010. Design and evaluation of an ontology based information extraction system for radiological reports. Comput. Biol. Med. 40, 11-12 (November 2010), 900-911.

Sang, E. T. K., Hofmann, K. 2009. Lexical patterns or dependency patterns: which is better for hypernym extraction?. In Proceedings of the Thirteenth Conference on Computational Natural Language Learning (CoNLL '09). Association for Computational Linguistics, Stroudsburg, PA, USA, 174-182.

Wimalasurya, D. C., Dou, D., Using Multiple Ontologies in Information Extraction.CIKM, 09, Hongkong, p.235-245, 2009. ACM Press.

Wyner, A. and Peterson, W. 2011. Rule Extraction from Regulations, The 24th International Conference on Legal Knowledge and Information Systems (Jurix).

Combined analysis of news and Twitter messages

Mian Du Jussi Kangasharju Ossi Karkulahti Lidia Pivovarova Roman Yangarber
University of Helsinki, Department of Computer Science

Abstract

While it is widely recognized that streams of social media messages contain valuable information, such as important trends in the users' interest in consumer products and markets, uncovering such trends is problematic, due to the extreme volumes of messages in such media. In the case Twitter messages, following the interest in relation to all known products all the time is technically infeasible. IE narrows topics to search. In this paper, we present experiments on using deeper NLP-based processing of product-related events mentioned in news streams to restrict the volume of tweets that need to be considered, to make the problem more tractable. Our goal is to analyze whether such a combined approach can help reveal correlations and how they may be captured.

1 Introduction

Twitter is a social networking and a micro-blogging service, that currently has more than 500 million users of which 200 million are using the service regularly. Many commercial organizations e.g. companies, newspapers and TV stations, as well as public entities, publish and promote their content through Twitter. According to the company itself, 60% of its users "access the service through mobile devices." On Twitter the relationships are by default directed, that is, user A can follow user B's posts without B following A. The posts on Twitter are referred to as tweets and at the moment of this writing there are more than 500 million tweets created daily. A tweet is limited to 140 characters of text, a legacy from the time when the system was envisioned to operate via SMS messages.

We will argue that our practice is not applicable to the Twitter service exclusively, however we elected to survey Twitter for a number of reasons. It has a huge number of users and is used worldwide. Because tweets are limited in length, the amount of data to be collected is kept manageable and it also helps maintain the analysis process simple. However, the most important factor for us was its openness. By default all tweets are public and the service offers a relatively functional and free API for gathering data.

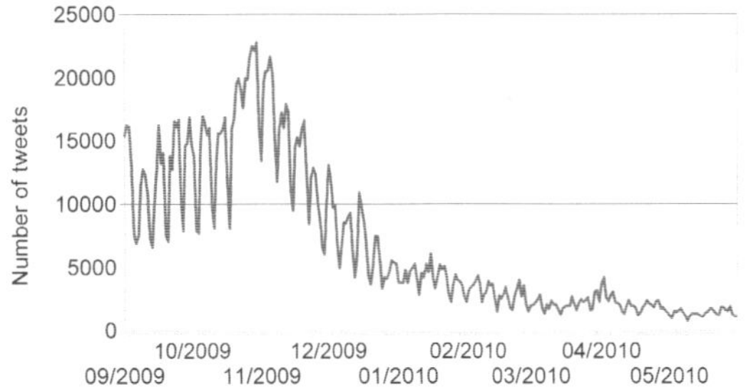

Figure 1: H1N1 on Twitter

Our earlier investigations demonstrate that Twitter users do react with higher volumes of posts to topical, news-worthy events. For instance, consider Figure 1, which plots the number of posts that contain keywords related to the 2009-2010 outbreak of H1N1 virus (swine flu). The curve matches almost perfectly with the peak of the outbreak and declines as the epidemic decayed. In this paper we will show that the topicality can be extended to business events, such as new product releases, and some releases indeed generate a large number of posts.

Until recently, a large part of research on social media has focused on analyzing and examining networks and graphs that emerge among users, references and links, and measuring patterns in creation and consumption of content. At present, more attention is being devoted to analyzing the vast volume of messages in the social media in terms of the *content* of the messages itself. Researchers in academia and industry are eager to mine the content for information that is not available from other sources, or before it becomes available from other sources (for example, see (Becker et al., 2012; Becker et al., 2011), and other works of the authors).

However, our work is not aimed at event discovery in Twitter. Instead, we try to discover how events, which we find in other sources—e.g., in traditional media—are presented on Twitter. We assume that it is worthy to know not only what kind of events can be found in Twitter but also events that are not present in tweets. For example, continuing the previous example, we can note that apart from flu there are many other diseases that can be less represented or completely absent from tweets.

From the point of view of natural language processing (NLP), the immediate problem that arises is that the linguistic register and language usage that is typical for social media content—such as web logs, and especially the ultra-short messages, such as those on Twitter—is very different from the register and usage in "traditional," well-studied sources of on-line textual information, such as news feeds. Therefore, it has been observed that new approaches are needed if we are to succeed raising the quality of analysis of the content of social media messages to useful levels. This territory remains largely uncharted, though the need is quite urgent, since a better understanding of the content will enable developments in areas such as market research and advertisement, and will also help improve the social media services themselves.

In this paper we examine how companies and products mentioned in the news are portrayed in message streams on the Twitter social networking service; in particular, we focus on media events related to the announcement or release of new products by companies. Our main research questions are: do interesting correlations exist between reports of a product release in the news and the volume of posts discussing the product on Twitter? Are some types of products more likely to generate more posts than others? Do different types of products trigger the generation of different types of messages?

One serious problem when conducting social media research is managing the data collection, and assuring that the system does not become overwhelmed with an enormous volume of data. In this paper we present a hybrid approach, where we first apply Information Extraction (IE) to messages found in news streams to narrow down scope of potentially relevant data that we will subsequently collect from Twitter. The volume of news is orders of magnitude smaller and more manageable than the volume of Twitter. In particular, extracting company and product names mentioned in the news will yield keywords that will match hot topics on Twitter. Although we may miss some important events on Twitter using this procedure, we reason that it is more tractable than continually keeping track of a large list of companies and products. An equally important factor is the fact that keeping lists of companies and products is not only impractical, but it is also insufficient, since new companies and novel products are introduced to the markets every day.

Our contributions and results include:

- we demonstrate how deeper NLP analysis can be used to help narrow down scope of messages to be retrieved from social-media message streams;

- we observe interesting correlations between events that are found in the two sources;

- we present some details about the content of tweets that correspond to news-worthy events: e.g., proportions retweeted messages and links, showing that sharing links is common when discussing certain products.

The remainder of the paper is structured as follows. Section 2 discusses related work. Section 3 describes the event extraction process, and covers the details of the data collection from Twitter. We discuss our results in Section 4, and Section 5 presents our conclusions and an outline of future work.

2 Related work

Research on social media, and on Twitter in particular, has been attracting increasing attention. It is a crucial source of information about public moods and opinions, for example, on topics of public concern such as political changes and elections (Diakopoulos and Shamma, 2010), or revolutions (Lotan et al., 2011). Twitter also can be useful for monitoring of natural disasters and epidemics of infectious disease (Lamb et al., 2013). At the same time, Twitter is a problematic source since traditional NLP methods for information extraction, opinion mining, etc., are not directly applicable to very short texts, or texts using communication styles peculiar to social media (Timonen et al., 2011).

Similar work to ours was reported by Tanev et al. (2012), who first used a fact extraction system to find events related to social unrest and cross-border criminal activity, and then tried to find additional information by using Twitter feeds. Becker et al. (2011) trained a classifier to distinguish tweets that relate to real-word events from tweets that do not. They demonstrate that event-related tweets are quite rare; the majority of tweets do not contain events.

Kwak et al. (2010) compared topics that attract major attention on Twitter with coverage in other sources, namely, Google Trends and CNN headlines. They have found that Twitter can be a source of breaking news as well. Zhao et al. (2011) used topic modelling to compare Twitter with the New York Times news site. They found Business as being among the top-10 topics on Twitter; however, business-related tweets rarely express opinions.

Krüger et al. (2012) manually analyzed 500 random tweets related to Adidas, and came to the conclusion that the company uses Twitter to promote their brand. Jansen et al. (2009) manually prepared a list of companies and brands belonging to different Business sectors, and then collected tweets related to these companies and brands. They demonstrate that approximately 20% of tweets contain mentions of companies or brands, which means that Twitter is an important marketing medium; however, only 20% of the tweets that mention companies and brands express a sentiment about them.

3 Data Collection

We use PULS[1] to extract events from text. PULS is a framework for discovering, aggregating, vizualization and verification of events in various domains, including Epidemics Surveillance, Cross-Border Security and Business.

In Business scenario events typically include merges and acquisitions, investments, layoffs,

On Friday, **Nokia** unveiled the **Lumia 928** for the **U.S.** market, priced at $99 after a rebate and a two-year deal with Verizon Wireless.

The Lumia 928 is the latest version in Nokia's range of **smartphones** using Windows Phone software, with its metal body setting it apart from earlier models.

COUNTRY:	US
DATE:	2013.05.10
COMPANY:	NOKIA
PRODUCT NAME:	Lumia 928
PRODUCT DESCRIPTION:	smartphone
SECTOR:	Telecommunications

Figure 2: A news text and a "New Product" event, extracted from this document by IE system.

nominations, etc. In this paper we focus on "New Product" events, i.e., when a company launches a new product or service on the market. Figure 2 presents an example of a piece of text from a news article and an event structure extracted from this text. A product event describes a company name, a product name, a location, a date, and the industry sector to which the event is related. These slots are filled by a combination of rule-based and supervised-learning approaches (Grishman et al., 2002; Yangarber, 2003; Huttunen et al., 2013).

For identifying the industry sectors to which the events relate, we use a classification system, currently containing 40 broad sectors, e.g., "Electronics," "Food," or "Transport." This classification system is similar to existing classification standards, such as the Global Industry Classification System (GICS),[2], or the Industry Classification Benchmark (ICB, http://www.icbenchmark.com/), with some simplifying modifications. The sector is assigned to the event using a Naive-Bayes classifier, which is trained on a manually-labeled set of news articles, approximately 200 for each sector, that we collected over several years.

We use the new-product events extracted by PULS to construct special queries to the Twitter API. One query contains a company name and a product name, which are the slots of a product event (see Figure 2). Every day we extract about 50 product events from news articles, and generate 50 corresponding queries to the Twitter API. We then use the Twitter API and collect all tweets that include both the company and the product name. Below one can see an example tweet containing the company name *Audi* and the product name *A3*:

[1]The Pattern Understanding and learning System: http://puls.cs.helsinki.fi

[2]http://www.msci.com/products/indices/sector/gics/

Time	Events	Tweets
Nov 2012–May 2013	1764	3,842,148

Table 1: Dataset description

`The new A3 from Audi looks great!`

The Twitter API has some restrictions. While conducting our survey[3], we could make 150 requests per hour, asking for 100 tweets per request, yielding a maximum of 15,000 tweets per hour. We had at our disposal the University of Helsinki cluster consisting of approximately machines, giving us the theoretical possibility to collect up to 3,000,000 tweets per hour.

While the company and product names are used as keywords in the Twitter query, other slots of the event are used for analyzing the results of the query. These slots, which include the industry sector, the country, the product description, and the date of the report, are used to label the tweets returned by the query. For example, we extract an event as in Figure 2 and get 2,000 tweets which contain both "Nokia" and "Lumia 928". Since the event is related to the industry sector "Telecommunications", we consider these 2,000 tweets are also related to "Telecommunications". Thus, we can group the returned tweets by industry sectors, country, etc., and analyze the flow of information.

The Twitter API lets us fetch tweets from seven previous days, and we kept collecting the tweets for each keyword for at least 3 days after its mention in the news. Thus, every keyword query has a time-line of roughly ten days around the news date.

The dataset is summarized in Table 1. We started the survey in November 2012 and the results presented in this paper include data collected through May 2013. In total, there are 1764 different events and in total close to 4 million tweets. In the final section of this paper we will discuss how we plan to improve the data collection in the future.

4 Experiments and results

4.1 Tweet statistics overview

First we present an overview of the tweet statistics. Table 2 summarizes the statistics, grouping the events based on the number of tweets they generated. The table also lists the total number of tweets, the percent of tweets that contain at least one hyper-link URL, and the percent of "retweets". A retweet is somewhat analogous to forwarding of an email. A retweets starts with "RT" abbreviation, making it easily distinguishable. Note that retweet can contain additional text compared to the original tweet, e.g., the retweeting user's personal opinion. The last column on the table represents the fraction of unique tweets; to count this number we subtracted from the total amount of tweets the number of tweets which were exactly identical. We pruned away the shortened link URLs from the tweet text when we calculated the uniqueness percentage, since the same URL can be shortened differently.

[3]The access conditions have been recently changed

Number of tweets	Number of events	Links %	Retweets %	Unique tweets %
10k+	33	82	22	52
1k-10k	68	78	23	53
100-1k	109	79	24	61
10-100	258	84	18	73
1-10	249	85	12	85

Table 2: Overall statistics: number of tweets, links and retweets per event

As can be seen from Table 2 there were 33 product events that generated more than 10,000 tweets. Strikingly, 82 percent of the tweets had a link. We checked a random sample through a subset of the tweets, and it seems that the single most common reason for the high number of links is that many websites today have a "share on Twitter" button, which allows a user to share a Web article with his/her followers by posting it on the user's Twitter page. The resulting tweet will have the article's original title, a generic description of the article (such as the one used in a RSS feed), and a link to the actual article. This can also be seen on the last column in Table 2, since the resulting tweets are always identical.

It is interesting to observe that the tweet uniqueness drops as the number of tweets increases. This would seem to indicate that the likelihood that an article is shared increases with the number of times it has already been shared. The same seems to hold for retweets as well. This corresponds to the observations found in literature: it was shown, (Kwak et al., 2010), that if a particular tweet has been retweeted once, it is likely that it will be retweeted again. Similarly, tweets that contain a URL are more likely to be retweeted (Suh et al., 2010). However, tweets related to business are rarely retweeted (Zhao et al., 2011).

COMPANY	# events	max # tweets	total # tweets
Facebook	13	444188	1931445
Microsoft	18	440831	447104
Google	24	410986	877842
Nokia	8	52955	60655
Nintendo	2	46611	75275
Apple	8	19619	42243
Lamborghini	1	21951	21951
Adobe	3	16230	17801
Lego	2	15371	26001
Audi	9	13373	13829
Netflix	2	9880	14249
Casio	1	8970	8970
Amazon	5	8678	10079
Huawei	5	8559	8906
Sony	12	8081	12459
T-Mobile	2	7884	9043
Adidas	13	6487	9171
Acer	1	6099	8592
Volkswagen	2	4454	4454
Subaru	1	4397	4397
Macklemore	1	4301	4301
Zynga	2	4166	4170
Starbucks	1	3993	3993
Lenovo	2	3129	3129
Land Rover	3	2951	4619
Seat	1	2641	2641
Walmart	1	2575	2575
Samsung Electronics	24	2566	4578
Chevrolet	2	2517	2558
Coca-Cola	23	2432	5891
Deezer	1	2107	2107
Tesla Motors	1	2082	2082
Macef	1	2073	2073
Telefonica	6	2065	2090
Orange	7	1958	2532
H&M	2	1787	1787
Dacia	2	1650	1849
Intel	2	1649	1649
Dell	2	1074	2450
Lacoste	2	799	821

Table 3: Most frequently tweeted companies

4.2 What is tweeted most frequently

The total number of distinct companies present in our data set is 1,140. The majority of these companies occur in one event only; for 50% of the companies less than 10 tweets have been returned. The list of most frequently tweeted companies is shown in Table 3. We show the number of events for a company in our dataset, the maximum number of tweets for any one event, and the total number of tweets for the company.

It can be seen from the table that only events related to well-known IT giants, (Facebook, Google, Microsoft), produce more than 100,000 tweets. Nokia, which is on the fourth position, produces 8 times fewer tweets than Google.[4]

SECTOR	events	max # tweets	total # tweets
Media, Information Services	109	444188	1534300
Telecommunications	122	337776	531920
Information Technology	33	169086	182408
Consumer Goods	41	15371	29440
Drinks	94	3993	10312
Automotive Engineering	66	4454	10098
Transport	36	1714	9570
Cosmetics & Chemicals	113	3480	6194
Food	106	4369	5751
Energy	6	277	374
Finance	45	179	316
Textiles	10	166	290
Health	25	81	239

Table 4: Most frequently tweeted industry sectors.

Other companies in table are telecommunication and automotive companies, food and drink producers, cosmetics and clothing suppliers. By contrast airlines receive little attention, the news about opening new flight routes cause little response on Twitter. For example, the only tweet related to a new flight by Air Baltic between Riga and Olbia was found in a Twitter account which is specialized for the airline's news.

The list of the most frequently tweeted industry sectors is shown in Table 4. Note, that the business sectors are assigned to events, not to a particular company; for example, an event that describes Facebook launched "Home," an operating system for mobile phones, was assigned with the sector "Telecommunications Technologies", while an event that describes that Facebook launched Graph Search was assigned with sector "Media, Information Services".

As can be seen from Table 4, the sectors in our data are distributed approximately according to Zipf's law: the majority of tweets are related to a limited number of sectors, while the majority of sectors trigger little or no response on Twitter. For example, we do not find any tweets related to such sectors as "Construction" or "Minerals & Metals"; the "Agriculture" sector generated only 3 tweets.

Comparing tables 4 and 3 we can observe that there is a dependency between the number of

[4]We have found relatively few tweets related to Samsung Electronics, even though these events are about launching new smartphones and other gadgets, which seem to be very popular in Twitter. We believe that we did not find more tweets because the full name of the company—"Samsung Electronics"—is rarely used in the tweets, which tend to refer to it as "Samsung;" this type of synonymy will be taken into account in future work. The majority of tweets related to Samsung are links to news (see an example in Figure 3); the text of these tweets are mostly identical (Figure 4), which means that people do not type new information but only click the "tweet" button on the news page.

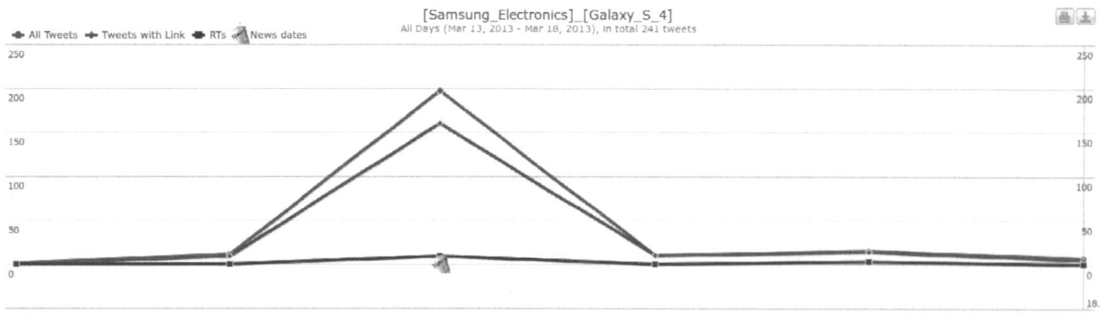

Figure 3: Number of tweets, links and retweets related to an event "Samsung Electronics launched Galaxy S4".

Timestamp (sort)	ID	Tweet	
2013-03-15T17:59:31	312624113040625665	How the Galaxy S 4 stacks up against iPhone, S III: Samsung Electronics Co. revealed its new top-of-the-line s... http://t.co/98XgVNyfpp	campus42
2013-03-15T17:59:11	312624028839981057	Noticias TNO Venezuela - Samsung presenta el GALAXY S 4: Samsung Electronics anunció hoy la cua... http://t.co/5iL3luXEJf #noticias #tno	Grupotno
2013-03-15T17:58:59	312623478605341696	How the Galaxy S 4 stacks up against iPhone, S III: Samsung Electronics Co. revealed its new top-of-the-line s... http://t.co/MzBzNoqzxa	World News
2013-03-15T17:56:57	312623465184235521	How the Galaxy S 4 stacks up against iPhone, S III: Samsung Electronics Co. revealed its new top-of-the-line s... http://t.co/aMFxz7ZmEC	SantinaMelgar
2013-03-15T17:56:54	312623455122124800	#TeamFollowBack How the Galaxy S 4 stacks up against iPhone, S III: Samsung Electronics Co. re... http://t.co/mLfYFHDsS4 #AutoFollowBack	Vermandita
2013-03-15T17:56:50	312623436721704961	#Tech How the Galaxy S 4 stacks up against iPhone, S III: Samsung Electronics Co. revealed its new top-of-the-... http://t.co/FzsjeQjllh	zankrut
2013-03-15T17:56:50	312623435819917312	How the Galaxy S 4 stacks up against iPhone, S III: Samsung Electronics Co. revealed it... http://t.co/nvVT1PXlYW http://t.co/jczlrGv4c1	Riyajain1
2013-03-15T17:56:48	312623429033553921	How the Galaxy S 4 stacks up against iPhone, S III: Samsung Electronics Co. revealed its new top-of-the-line s... http://t.co/nKRRFRzqRn	technewsplace
2013-03-15T17:56:46	312623421320216578	How the Galaxy S 4 stacks up against iPhone, S III: Samsung Electronics Co. revealed its new top-of-the-line s... http://t.co/EgvCvVMNgR	drGalauuu
2013-03-15T17:56:44	312623412621213697	How the Galaxy S 4 stacks up against iPhone, S III: Samsung Electronics Co. revealed its new top-of-the-line... http://t.co/GbSS116OHA	TomFlowers

Figure 4: Tweets related to an event "Samsung Electronics launched Galaxy S4".

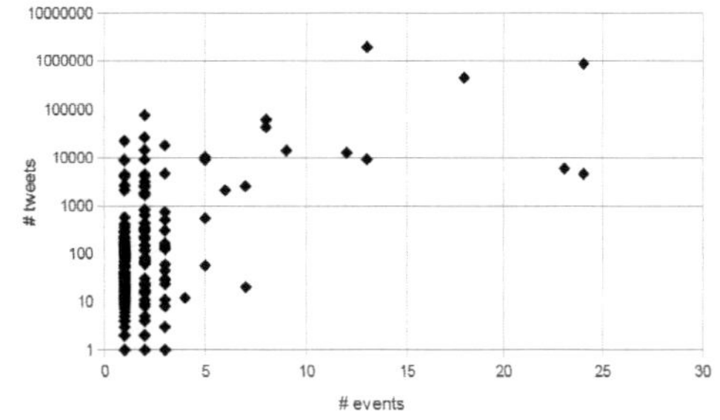

Figure 5: Number of events against total number of tweets for companies.

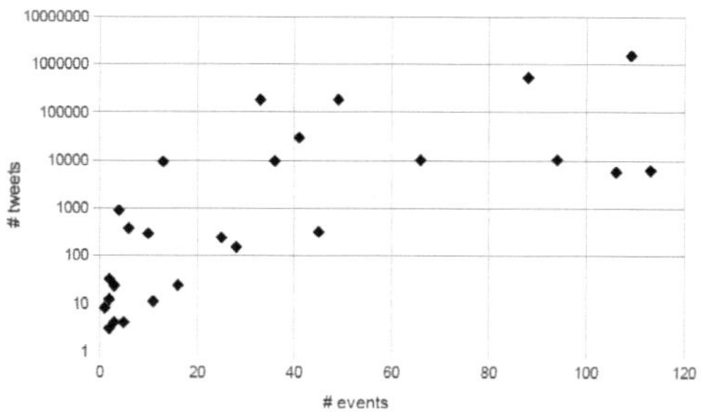

Figure 6: Number of events against total number of tweets for sectors.

events related to a particular sector and the number of tweets related to this sector, whereas there seems to be no such relation between the number of events related to particular company and a number of tweets related to this company. For example, only one event involving Acer appeared during the covered period—a launch of the "Iconia B1" tablet—but it drew more than 6,000 tweets.

The dependencies between the number of events and the number of tweets for companies and sectors are presented in Figures 5 and 6 respectively.

All events were taken from news written in English, but depending on the resulting keywords, the tweets that match the query could be in any language. Since we use the English names for companies and products there is an inherent bias toward countries that use languages with a Latin-based script. However, despite that were able to find many tweets for events that happen in countries that use non-Latin scripts, e.g., Russia or Japan. Two reasons for this may be that the larger companies operates globally, and that Twitter users tend to type company and product names in English even though they tweet in their own languages, see examples in Figure 7.

2013-04-22T23:59:41	326485492078003328	みんなGoogle Glass好きなんやなぁ	mowsmow
2013-04-22T23:59:41	326485490150817793	RT @ragemax: Google Glassで拓かれる未来 Glassユーザー「百合カップルきたあああああ」 フォロワー「画像もなしに...」 Glassユーザー「しょうがないなあ、視覚共有してやるよ」 フォロワー「うおおおおおおおお！！！！！1」 こういう未来ですか？	maxonK
2013-04-22T23:59:40	326485486585655297	RT @ragemax: Google Glassで拓かれる未来 Glassユーザー「百合カップルきたあああああ」 フォロワー「画像もなしに...」 Glassユーザー「しょうがないなあ、視覚共有してやるよ」 フォロワー「うおおおおおおおお！！！！！1」 こういう未来ですか？	matoriv
2013-04-22T23:59:40	326485485310595074	エロがなければ映像ソフトの発展はなかったように エロがなければ革命的デバイスの発展も望めないのだ だからGoogle Glassがラッキースケベ共有のために使われるのは 極めて自然である	ragemax
2013-04-22T23:59:38	326485478796832768	RT @ragemax: Google Glassで拓かれる未来 Glassユーザー「百合カップルきたあああああ」 フォロワー「画像もなしに...」 Glassユーザー「しょうがないなあ、視覚共有してやるよ」 フォロワー「うおおおおおおおお！！！！！1」 こういう未来ですか？	Miyata_Iori
2013-04-22T23:59:38	326485477521764352	RT @latercera: Google Glass utilizará pestañeos para sacar fotografías y los dedos para hacer zoom http://t.co/7mCIuWBIWp	armagonttboy361
2013-04-22T23:59:37	326485475185537025	RT @ragemax: Google Glassが買えても きっと日本人ならろくでもない使い方しか思いつかないに違いない	uninosuke
2013-04-22T23:59:31	326485450359459840	Google Glass、どうせシャッター音消せないんだろ？意味ねえな	jieigumin
2013-04-22T23:59:31	326485448346198017	【速報】Google glassすごすぎｗｗｗｗｗｗｗｗｗ http://t.co/xKGlqeP9yg	asahirovip

Figure 7: Tweets related to an event "Google launched Google Glass".

5 Conclusion and future work

We described an end-to-end framework, which allows us to analyze the influence that business news have on tweets. We have demonstrated that the impact that new-product events have on Twitter depends more on the industry sector than on a particular company. It is clear, however, that the developed framework can be used in more broad applications, at least for more sophisticated data analysis.

Our data, as it was shown before, include the event date and the timestamps for tweets. However, in the current paper this data have been overlooked in the analysis. Thus, the main direction of the further work will focus more on the temporal dimension. We are going to add more metrics, such as the time gap between the product launch and the peak of tweets.

Furthermore, we would like to see whether we could predict the impact created by a product launch based on the history and to find out if there are some models to match that and the lifetime of the tweets. To solve this problem, we plan to modify our data collection process and to monitor a several big companies for a longer time, in order to establish baselines. This will allows us, first, to analyze the exact impact of a product launch on Twitter volume and, second, to measure an impact of corpus narrowing using IE.

Another aspect of the data, which would be interesting to investigate, is location. As have been shown before, the business events include a country slot; however, we cannot assume that corresponding tweets originate from the same country. Thus, we are going to use geolocation techniques, (Dredze et al., 2013; Bergsma et al., 2013), to find the tweets' countries and to compare them with the countries found in news.

We also plan to improve the query construction algorithm to find more tweets for compound company names, such as "Samsung Electronics." This cannot be done in a straightforward fashion: "Samsung" may likely refer to "Samsung Electronics", though "Electronics" may refer to many different entities. Thus we cannot simply search for all substrings of a company name, because such queries will produce to many false hits. We assume that special named entity recognition techniques, which have been recently developed for Twitter (Ritter et al., 2011; Piskorski and Ehrmann, 2013), can be used to solve this problem. To improve coverage it is also possible to use automatic transliteration, which allows to map proper names from Latin to other scripts (Nouri et al., 2013).

We have studied the most and least frequently tweeted companies and industry sectors. In the next phases we will study the most frequently tweeted product types. Since every product found by IE system has a description (as presented in Figure 2), we can group tweets by product type. However, additional work is needed to merge such product types as, for example, "chocolate" and "chocolate candies". We plan to use a Business concept ontology, which includes the long list of possible product types, to perform this task.

References

Hila Becker, Mor Naaman, and Luis Gravano. 2011. Beyond trending topics: Real-world event identification on Twitter. In *International Conference on Weblogs and Social Media*, Barcelona, Spain.

Hila Becker, Dan Iter, Mor Naaman, and Luis Gravano. 2012. Identifying content for planned events across social media sites. In *The fifth ACM international conference on Web search and data mining*, pages 533–542, Seattle, Washington.

Shane Bergsma, Mark Dredze, Benjamin Van Durme,

Theresa Wilson, and David Yarowsky. 2013. Broadly improving user classification via communication-based name and location clustering on Twitter. In *North American Chapter of the Association for Computational Linguistics (NAACL)*, Atlanta, Georgia.

Nicholas A. Diakopoulos and David A. Shamma. 2010. Characterizing debate performance via aggregated Twitter sentiment. In *Proceedings of the 28th international conference on Human factors in computing systems*, pages 1195–1198. ACM.

Mark Dredze, Michael J. Paul, Shane Bergsma, and Hieu Tran. 2013. Carmen: a Twitter geolocation system with applications to public health. In *AAAI Workshop on Expanding the Boundaries of Health Informatics Using AI (HIAI)*.

Ralph Grishman, Silja Huttunen, and Roman Yangarber. 2002. Event extraction for infectious disease outbreaks. In *Proc. 2nd Human Language Technology Conf. (HLT 2002)*, San Diego, CA.

Silja Huttunen, Arto Vihavainen, Mian Du, and Roman Yangarber. 2013. Predicting relevance of event extraction for the end user. In *Multi-source, Multilingual Information Extraction and Summarization*, Theory and Applications of Natural Language Processing, pages 163–176. Springer Berlin.

Bernard J. Jansen, Mimi Zhang, Kate Sobel, and Abdur Chowdury. 2009. Twitter power: tweets as electronic word of mouth. *Journal of the American Society for Information Science and Technology*, 60(11):2169–2188.

Nina Krüger, Stefan Stieglitz, and Tobias Potthoff. 2012. Brand communication in Twitter—a case study on Adidas. In *PACIS 2012 Proceedings*.

Haewoon Kwak, Changhyun Lee, Hosung Park, and Sue Moon. 2010. What is Twitter, a social network or a news media? In *Proceedings of the 19th international conference on World wide web*, pages 591–600. ACM.

Alex Lamb, Michael J. Paul, and Mark Dredze. 2013. Separating fact from fear: Tracking flu infections on Twitter. In *Proceedings of NAACL-HLT*, pages 789–795.

Gilad Lotan, Erhardt Graeff, Mike Ananny, Devin Gaffney, Ian Pearce, and Danah Boyd. 2011. The revolutions were tweeted: Information flows during the 2011 Tunisian and Egyptian revolutions. *International Journal of Communication*, 5:1375–1405.

Javad Nouri, Lidia Pivovarova, and Roman Yangarber. 2013. MDL-based models for transliteration generation. In *SLSP 2013: International Conference on Statistical Language and Speech Processing*, Tarragona, Spain.

Jakub Piskorski and Maud Ehrmann. 2013. On named entity recognition in targeted Twitter streams in Polish. In *The 4th Biennial International Workshop on Balto-Slavic Natural Language Processing : ACL 2013*, pages 84–93, Sofia, Bulgaria.

Alan Ritter, Sam Clark, Oren Etzioni, et al. 2011. Named entity recognition in tweets: an experimental study. In *Proceedings of the Conference on Empirical Methods in Natural Language Processing*, pages 1524–1534. Association for Computational Linguistics.

Bongwon Suh, Lichan Hong, Peter Pirolli, and Ed H. Chi. 2010. Want to be retweeted? Large scale analytics on factors impacting retweet in Twitter network. In *Social Computing (SocialCom), 2010 IEEE Second International Conference on*, pages 177–184. IEEE.

Hristo Tanev, Maud Ehrmann, Jakub Piskorski, and Vanni Zavarella. 2012. Enhancing event descriptions through Twitter mining. In *Sixth International AAAI Conference on Weblogs and Social Media*, pages 587–590.

Mika Timonen, Paula Silvonen, and Melissa Kasari. 2011. Classification of short documents to categorize consumer opinions. In *Proccedings of 7th International Conference on Advanced Data Mining and Applications*, pages 1–14.

Roman Yangarber. 2003. Counter-training in discovery of semantic patterns. In *Proc. ACL-2003*, Sapporo, Japan.

Wayne Xin Zhao, Jing Jiang, Jianshu Weng, Jing He, Ee-Peng Lim, Hongfei Yan, and Xiaoming Li. 2011. Comparing Twitter and traditional media using topic models. In *Advances in Information Retrieval*, pages 338–349. Springer.

Linguistically analyzed labels of knowledge objects: How can they support OBIE? Lessons learned from the Monnet and TrendMiner projects

Thierry Declerck
DFKI GmbH
thierry.declerck@dfki.de

1 Abstract

We are investigating the use of natural language expressions included in Knowledge Organization Systems (KOS) for supporting Ontology-Based Information Extraction (OBIE), in a multi- and cross-lingual context.

Very often, Knowledge Organization Systems include so-called annotation properties, in the form of *labels*, *comments*, *definitions*, etc, which have the purpose of introducing human readable information in the formal description of the domain modelled in the KOS.

An approach developed in the Monnet project, and continued in the TrendMiner project, consists in transforming the content of annotation properties into linguistically analysed data. Natural language processing of such language expressions, also called sometimes *lexicalisation* of Knowledge Organisation Systems, are thus transforming the unstructured content of annotation properties into linguistically structured data, which can be used in comparing language data included in a KOS with linguistically annotated texts. If some match of linguistic features between those two types of documents can be established, corresponding segments of the textual documents can be semantically annotated with the elements of the KOS the content of the annotation property is associated with. Evidently, this semantic annotation procedure can be of great help for OBIE, relating text segment to relevant parts of thesauri, taxonomy or ontologies.

But looking in more details at the language data contained in annotation properties, we can see that this data very often has to be modified in order to be better used in the context of OBIE. Also there is a need for a formal representation of such linguistically annotated language data in order to ensure interoperability with semantic data available in the Linked Data Framework.

The talk will expand on those issues.

2 Short Bio

Thierry Declerck is senior consultant at DFKI's LT lab and he was leading the DFKI contribution to the European Project MONNET[1]. Before this he was in charge of the DFKI contribution to the Integrated Project MUSING[2], which finished in April 2010, and till March 2009 he was involved as well in the European Network of Excellence "K-Space" (*Knowledge Space of semantic inference for automatic annotation and retrieval of multimedia content*). In the field of standardization of language resources, Thierry Declerck was involved in the eContent "Lirics" (Linguistic Infrastructure for Interoperable Resources and Systems) project (see http://lirics.loria.fr/) and was leading the MUMIS project on the Indexing and Search of Multimedia data. He was also in charge of the ACL Natural Language Software Registry, which is now integrated in lt-world. Since Mai 2004, he was conducting the DFKI contribution of the eTen WINS project. Thierry Declerck is also actively involved in ISO TC37/SC4/ (on language resources management).

[1] http://www.monnet-project.eu/
[2] http://www.musing.eu/

Author Index